A Note From Rick Renner

I am on a personal quest to see a "revival of the Bible" so people can establish their lives on a firm foundation that will stand strong and endure the test when the end-time storm winds begin to intensify.

In order to experience a revival of the Bible in your personal life, it is important to take time each day to read, receive, and apply its truths to your life. James tells us that if we will continue in the perfect law of liberty — refusing to be forgetful hearers but determined to be doers — we will be blessed in our ways. As you watch or listen to the programs in this series and work through this corresponding study guide, I trust that you will search the Scriptures and allow the Holy Spirit to help you hear something new from God's Word that applies specifically to your life. I encourage you to be a doer of the Word that He reveals to you. Whatever the cost, I assure you — it will be worth it.

Thy words were found, and I did eat them;
and thy word was unto me the joy and rejoicing of mine heart:
for I am called by thy name, O Lord God of hosts.
—Jeremiah 15:16

Your brother and friend in Jesus Christ,

Rick Renner

Unless otherwise indicated, all scripture quotations are taken from the *King James Version* of the Bible.

Scripture quotations marked (*AMPC*) are taken from the *Amplified® Bible Classic Edition*, copyright © 1954, 1958, 1962, 1964, 1965, 1987 by The Lockman Foundation. Used by permission. **www.Lockman.org**.

Scripture quotations marked (*NKJV*) are taken from the *New King James Version®*. Copyright © 1982 by Thomas Nelson. Used by permission. All rights reserved.

Dressed To Kill

8316 E. 73rd St.
Tulsa, Oklahoma 74133

Published by Rick Renner Ministries
www.renner.org

ISBN 13: 978-1-68031-833-3

eBook ISBN 13: 978-1-68031-834-0

How To Use This Study Guide

This ten-lesson study guide corresponds to ***"Dressed To Kill" With Rick Renner*** **(Renner TV)**. Each lesson in this study guide covers a topic that is addressed during the program series, with questions and references supplied to draw you deeper into your own private study of the Scriptures on this subject.

To derive the most benefit from this study guide, consider the following:

First, watch or listen to the program prior to working through the corresponding lesson in this guide. (Programs can also be viewed at **renner.org** by clicking on the Media/Archives links.)

Second, take the time to look up the scriptures included in each lesson. Prayerfully consider their application to your own life.

Third, use a journal or notebook to make note of your answers to each lesson's Study Questions and Practical Application challenges.

Fourth, invest specific time in prayer and in the Word of God to consult with the Holy Spirit. Write down the scriptures or insights He reveals to you.

Finally, take action! Whatever the Lord tells you to do according to His Word, do it.

For added insights on this subject, it is recommended that you obtain Rick Renner's book ***Dressed To Kill: A Biblical Approach to Spiritual Warfare and Armor***. You may also select from Rick's other available resources by placing your order at **renner.org** or by calling 1-800-742-5593.

TOPIC

Be Strong in the Lord

SCRIPTURES

1. **Ephesians 6:10** — Finally, my brethren, be strong in the Lord and in the power of his might.

GREEK WORDS

1. "Finally" — **Τοῦ λοιποῦ** (*Tou loipou*): for the rest of the matter; finally, to the last and most important matter at hand
2. "brethren" — **ἀδελφός** (*adelphos*): a term used to describe two or more who were born from the same womb; later used in a military sense to depict brothers in battle; a comrade; hence, brotherhood
3. "strong" — **ἐνδυναμόω** (*endunamoo*): compound of **ἐν** (*en*) and **δυναμόω** (*dunamoo*), which is from **δύναμις** (*dunamis*); the word **ἐν** (*en*) means into, such as in placing water into a vessel, and **δύναμις** (*dunamis*) means power; the word *dunamis* depicted the forces of an entire army; but when these words are compounded, it pictures the power of a whole army being deposited into a person; inner strengthening; supernatural enablement; pictures explosive, superhuman power that comes with enormous energy and produces phenomenal, extraordinary, and unparalleled results being deposited into a receptacle
4. "power" — **κράτος** (*kratos*): strength, power, victory over something, taking something by force, or storming something; demonstrated power; **κράτος** (*kratos*) is not a power that you merely adhere to and believe in intellectually, but is a power that is demonstrative, eruptive, and tangible
5. "might" — **ἰσχύος** (*ischuos*): a strong man, such as a mighty man with great muscular capabilities; used in the New Testament to picture God as One who is able, mighty, and muscular; one with all the might and ability to overcome any foe or to accomplish any act needed; power, strength, great might, great force, or great ability

SYNOPSIS

The ten lessons in this study entitled ***Dressed To Kill*** will focus on the following topics:

- Be Strong in the Lord
- The Whole Armor of God
- The Devil, Who He Is and What He Does
- The Wiles, Devices, and Deception of the Devil
- Wrestling With Principalities and Powers
- The Champion God Sees You To Be
- The Loinbelt of Truth, Breastplate of Righteousness
- The Shoes of Peace and Shield of Faith
- The Helmet of Salvation, Sword of the Spirit, Lance of Prayer
- Pulling Down Strongholds

The emphasis of this lesson:

Before the apostle Paul revealed the spiritual weapons we have been given by God, he urged us to "be strong in the Lord." Only when the all-surpassing power of the Holy Spirit is released within us are we dressed in our armor and empowered to deal victoriously with the archenemy of our faith.

Located in the Winter Palace and Hermitage Museum complex in Saint Petersburg, Russia, is a vast collection of armor. It was started by Emperor Alexander I, and it has grown enormously over the years. As a matter of fact, it now contains more than 15,000 pieces of armor and weaponry, most of which are of the European variety.

Did you know that God has provided you with spiritual weapons? It's true. God has given you spiritual weaponry to cover you from head to toe, but in order for you to be able to carry your weapons and put them to use, you have to be spiritually strong. You need the supernatural power of God filling and empowering you to face and defeat the enemy's attacks.

Paul Saved the Most Important Thing for Last

In the second half of Ephesians 6, the apostle Paul began his teaching on the armor of God. But just before he gets into the description of each piece of our weaponry, he urges us to receive the supernatural power of God.

> **"Finally, my brethren, be strong in the Lord and in the power of his might."**
>
> **Ephesians 6:10**

Take note of the word "finally." It is a translation of the Greek word *Tou loipou*, which means *for the rest of the matter*, or it could be translated as, "*Finally, to the last and most important matter at hand.*" The reason the use of this word is so significant is because Paul introduced and talked about several very important concepts of the Christian faith in the book of Ephesians. For example:

- In **Ephesians 1**, he discussed the blessing of being chosen by God and being predestined to be conformed to the image of Christ. He also talked about us being sealed with the Holy Spirit and receiving the earnest of the Spirit as a down payment of our full redemption that is coming.
- In **Ephesians 2**, he expounded on the extravagant grace and mercy of God.
- In **Ephesians 3**, he unveiled the eternal plan of God in the Church.
- In **Ephesians 4**, he explained Christ's gift of fivefold ministry.
- In **Ephesians 5**, he urged us to be filled with the Holy Spirit.
- In **Ephesians 6**, he opened the chapter by teaching on interpersonal relationships.

Then, after discussing all of these vital concepts, Ephesians 6:10 begins by saying, "Finally," which in the Greek means, "Finally, to the last and most important matter at hand. If you don't remember anything else I've said in this letter, please remember this, because I saved the most important thing to the very end. Be strong in the Lord and in the power of His might."

Why would Paul emphasize to the Ephesian believers that spiritual armor was so important? The reason is because they were in trouble. Even though they had a lot of spiritual knowledge and insight, we can see from

Ephesians 4 that they were grieving the Holy Spirit by gossiping, backbiting, and harboring malice and bitterness in their hearts. They were not behaving like victorious Christians and needed the power of God to come up higher in their way of living.

We Are All Fellow Fighters in the Faith

Next, notice how Paul addressed the Ephesian believers. He said, "Finally, my *brethren*..." (Ephesians 6:10). In Greek, the word "brethren" is *adelphos*, which is *a term used to describe two or more who were born from the same womb*. Later, it was used in a military sense to depict *brothers in battle*; *a comrade*; *hence, brotherhood*. That is where the word "brother" in the New Testament came from.

What is interesting is that the Greek word *adelphos* — translated here as "brethren" — was not popularized the way we use it in the Church today, until the time of Alexander the Great. History records that Alexander was the greatest soldier of all time, and every soldier wanted to be affiliated with him. So, from time to time he would hold extravagant awards ceremonies, calling each of his faithful soldiers to the stage. One by one, he would honor each man who had fought bravely. There in front of all the others, Alexander the Great would put his arms around each of them and say, "Let all the empire know that Alexander is proud to be the *adelphos* — the brother — of this soldier." This imagery became inseparably linked to the meaning of the word "brother" in New Testament times.

Therefore, when you call someone a *brother*, you are calling him a *comrade* or *a fellow fighter* in the faith. Despite any struggles they may have, they are still in the fight, and therefore you're proud to be associated with them. That is what the apostle Paul was saying to his fellow Ephesian believers. "Finally, to the last and most important matter at hand, my brothers in battle and fellow comrades I am so proud of, be strong in the Lord."

God Designed Us As Receptacles of His Explosive Power

When Paul told his fellow warriors to "be strong," he used the Greek word *endunamoo*. It is a compound of the words *en* and *dunamoo*, which is a form of the word *dunamis*. The word *en* means *into*, such as *in placing water into a vessel*. The very nature of this word *en* emphatically means that there must be some type of receiver for this power to be deposited into.

The word *dunamis* means *power*. Specifically, the word *dunamis* depicted *the forces of an entire invading army*. It was also used to describe *a force of nature*, such as a hurricane, a tornado, or an earthquake.

The word *dunamis* is the word used in Acts 1:8 to describe the power of the Holy Spirit that descended in the Upper Room on the Day of Pentecost and filled the 120 followers of Jesus with the dynamic power of God. Therefore, we could say that the Holy Spirit is like a divine force of nature that comes like a hurricane, a tornado, or an earthquake to transform the landscape and shake things up. When the Holy Spirit arrives on the scene, the full might of Heaven's army moves into action.

Thus, when Paul said, "Be strong," and used the word *endunamoo* — the compound of the words *en* and *dunamis* — it pictures *the power of a whole army being deposited into a person*. It describes *inner strengthening* or *supernatural enablement*. It pictures *explosive, superhuman power that comes with enormous energy and produces phenomenal, extraordinary, and unparalleled results being deposited into a receptacle*.

This is where we come into the picture! We are specially designed by God to be the receptacles for His divine power. The word *endunamoo* does not describe a free-floating power that drifts through the universe. It is divine, explosive power given by God, and according to Ephesians 6:10, we are the receptacles into which this power is to be deposited.

We Are Commanded To Receive His Transforming Power

Equally important to note is the Greek tense used in this verse. It is the present passive imperative tense. This means Paul was not simply suggesting that they receive this power; he was *commanding* them in the strongest of words to receive it — and to receive it as soon as possible. He was urging them — and all believers — to open their hearts to receive a brand-new touch of God's power into their lives.

In addition to the present imperative tense, Paul also used the passive tense in his command to "be strong." And the passive tense describes the ongoing, lasting effect of this power upon a believer's life. This tense tells us that, although there is an immediate strengthening effect when God's special *endunamoo* power is released in a believer's life, it is more than a one-shot experience. It is a supernatural power that continues to strengthen that believer for a long, long time to come.

Furthermore, the word *endunamoo,* translated as "strong," was frequently used by classical Greek writers to describe individuals who had been handpicked by the gods to perform extra-special, superhuman tasks. For instance, classical Greek writers would have said such superhuman strength was the result of the pagan gods depositing *endunamoo* power into him.

Paul was an exceptionally brilliant and educated man. From his own studies in classical Greek, he undoubtedly knew this historical usage of the word *endunamoo.* So when discussing the supernatural power that the Holy Spirit gives us to withstand the work of the adversary, Paul chose this word that had unmistakable connotations to denote a power that turns mere men into champions who possess superhuman, supernatural strength.

We Are Only Strong 'In the Lord'

Again, Paul said, "Finally, my brethren, be strong *in the Lord…*" (Ephesians 6:10). The supernatural power of God can only be obtained *in the Lord.* It cannot be obtained by reading books, attending conferences, or listening to teaching series. These are all well and good and have their place. But God's power is locked up in the Person of Jesus Christ.

This is actually great news for us because as believers, we are locked up in Christ! Actually multiple times in Ephesians 1 we are told that we are "in Christ." We read this in verses 3, 4, 6, 7, 10, 11, 12, and 13, and in Him is this divine, superhuman power. That means as we abide in a personal relationship with Jesus, we're rubbing elbows with the power of God 24 hours a day! Although we may not always be mentally aware of it, the very fact that both we and this special power are locked up "in the Lord" means we are never far away from a fresh surge of superhuman power into our own human spirits.

You are as close to this power as you are to breathing your next breath of air. You are in Christ, and in Christ is this power. It is yours for the taking. But it is not something you can earn or be good enough to receive. The infilling of the Holy Spirit is a work of grace and not of human effort.

God knew that He had to make it simple for us to receive His power. Otherwise, the majority of us would never receive it. Knowing this about us, God permanently "locked up" His power inside the Person of Jesus Christ, and He "locked us up" in Christ as well. By doing this for us, God placed us in a position to rub elbows with His divine power continuously. He graciously fixed it so it would be very difficult for us not to freely receive this impartation of superhuman, supernatural strength for the fight.

To experience God's ever-available, ever-accessible power, you must open your heart to it and ask that it be released in your life. Simply say, "Father, I reach out by faith and receive this special divine power right now." Again, because of your position "in the Lord," you are surrounded by His power right now. At this precise moment, you are immersed in God's supernatural power. *It is yours for the taking!* The only prerequisite to receive this power is that you are "in the Lord."

The Evidence Is Displayed in 'Power'

So, how can we tell when God's supernatural strength is operating in our lives? The apostle Paul answers this question in the latter part of Ephesians 6:10. He says, "Finally, my brethren, be strong in the Lord, and in the power of his might." Notice the words "power" and "might." Since they are listed separately in this verse, they must mean two different things.

First, we have the word "power," which is the Greek word *kratos*. It depicts *strength, power, or victory over something*. It means *taking something by force or storming something*. It is *demonstrated power*. In other words, *kratos* is not a power that you merely adhere to and believe in intellectually, but *a power that is demonstrative, eruptive, and tangible.*

This tells us that when we are "strong in the Lord" — when we're infused with the supernatural power that Paul is talking about in Ephesians 6:10 — it comes with real, tangible results. It is not hypothetical power; it is power you can feel and see at work with your own eyes. When that divine power comes and is operating in us, it wants to manifest. That is why when people are baptized in the Holy Spirit, they immediately want to see signs and wonders. They have received *kratos* power that wants to get out and visibly manifest.

Consider how invincible, overpowering, conquering, and irresistible that power was when it flooded the grave where Jesus' dead body lay. The resurrection power of God literally permeated every dead cell and fiber of Jesus' body with divine life — until it was impossible for death to hold Him!

If you had been at Jesus' tomb on resurrection morning, you wouldn't have just intellectually said, "Yes, I believe God's power came into the tomb." You would have physically felt the ground shake as the *kratos* power of God entered the tomb where Jesus' body lay. Then you would have watched as this *kratos* power raised Jesus from the dead! The *kratos* power is so overwhelming that the mighty Roman soldiers who were guarding Jesus' tomb on resurrection morning fainted and crumbled to the ground beneath the full load of this supernatural force. That is the kind of power that we have received.

When the empowering presence of the Holy Spirit is operative in our lives, it releases in us the same power that physically raised Jesus Christ from the dead. This *kratos* power is an eruptive, demonstrative, outwardly visible and manifested kind of power — the kind that we can see and experience.

Paul knew that before he began discussing the armor of God and warfare with unseen forces, first he had to cover the issue of power. Why? Because without this power operating in our spiritual lives, we can't engage in battle with the enemy. There is no way we can stand against the deeds of darkness in our own strength — it's an impossibility. Furthermore, we do not have the strength in ourselves to carry the heavy armor of God we so desperately need in our campaign against the wiles of the devil.

Now you may be thinking, *How is "power" different than "might"?* The word "might" in this verse is the Greek word *ischuos*, which describes *a strong man, such as a mighty man with great muscular capabilities*. This word is used in the New Testament to picture God as One who is able, mighty, and muscular. He is One with all the might and ability to overcome any foe or to accomplish any act needed. This word *ischuos* — translated here as "might" — means p*ower, strength, great might, great force, or great ability*.

- With one stroke of God's mighty arm, such a powerful force was discharged that the civilized world of Noah's day was flooded, and an entire period of civilization was wiped out.

- With one stroke of God's mighty arm, such overwhelming power was released that the cities of Sodom and Gomorrah were forever wiped off the face of the earth by fire and brimstone.
- With one stroke of God's mighty arm, the turbulent, raging Red Sea walls of water collapsed and came tumbling down to swallow up the pursuing chariots of Pharaoh.
- With one stroke of God's mighty arm, power surged into the grave and ripped Jesus out of the pangs of death, stripping principalities and powers naked and making a public display of their embarrassing defeat.

Today this same mighty arm of God is still working throughout the earth in you and all believers! One expositor translates Ephesians 6:10 in this way...

> **Be strong in the Lord and in the powerful, outwardly demonstrated ability that works in you as a result of God's great muscular ability.**

Friend, all that God is — all the power He possesses and all the energy of His muscular and mighty ability — energizes the *kratos* power that is at work in believers who have been empowered by the Holy Spirit. And if you want to defeat the devil and function in spiritual armor, you must first receive this divine power that is essential for the fight!

STUDY QUESTIONS

Study to shew thyself approved unto God, a workman that needeth not to be ashamed, rightly dividing the word of truth.
— 2 Timothy 2:15

1. When Paul wrote to the Ephesian believers, they were struggling in certain areas of their Christian life. Carefully read these informative passages and identify what issues they were dealing with and what Paul was encouraging them to cultivate in their lives.
   - Ephesians 4:1-6
   - Ephesians 4:17-24
   - Ephesians 4:25-32

2. The Greek word for "brother" used in the New Testament is *adelphos*, and it depicts *brothers in battle*, *a comrade*, or *a fellow fighter in the faith*. Who do you know that you're sincerely proud to call a "brother" (*adelphos*) in the faith? If you've never taken the time to express your appreciation for this person, look for an opportunity to purposely do so. In fact, pray and ask God to make a way for you to publically praise them for all that they have invested in your life.

PRACTICAL APPLICATION

But be ye doers of the word, and not hearers only, deceiving your own selves.
—James 1:22

1. God has fashioned you to be a receptacle of His divine power! Through the apostle Paul, He urges you to open your heart and receive a brand-new touch of His supernatural power. Have you ever received this supernatural empowerment from God — the baptism in the Holy Spirit? If so, describe your experience.
2. If you have not received God's supernatural empowerment but would like to, take a few moments to pray. Ask the Lord to forgive you and cleanse you of any sin you've committed. By faith, receive His forgiveness and ask Him to baptize you in the Holy Spirit! (To learn more about receiving this indescribable gift, read what Jesus said in Luke 11:9-13.)
3. Although there is an immediate strengthening effect when God's special *endunamoo* power is released in your life, it is more than a one-shot experience. It is a supernatural power that continues to strengthen you as a believer your entire life. To keep the fire of God burning brightly inside you, develop the healthy habit of asking God to release His ever-accessible power in you — and the habit of regularly praying in the prayer language of the Holy Spirit. You will be simply amazed at the far-reaching effects of this practice!

TOPIC

The Whole Armor of God

SCRIPTURES

1. **Ephesians 6:11** — Put on the whole armour of God, that ye may be able to stand against the wiles of the devil

GREEK WORDS

1. "put on"— **ἐνδύω** (*enduo*): compound of **ἐν** (*en*) and **δύναμις** (*dunamis*); the word **ἐν** (*en*) means into, such as in placing water into a vessel, and **δύναμις** (*dunamis*) means power; the word *dunamis* depicts the forces of an entire army; but when these words are compounded, it pictures the power of a whole army being deposited into a person; inner strengthening; supernatural enablement; pictures explosive, superhuman power that comes with enormous energy and produces phenomenal, extraordinary, and unparalleled results being deposited into a receptacle
2. "whole armour"— **πανοπλία** (*panoplia*): pictures a soldier fully dressed in his armor from head to toe; the full attire and weaponry of a soldier; though not all-inclusive, the following hardware was required for a soldier to be fully dressed for battle: the loinbelt, breastplate, shoes, shield, helmet, sword, and lance
3. "to stand"— **στῆναι** (*stenai*): to stand upright

SYNOPSIS

If you were to visit the Winter Palace and the Hermitage complex in Saint Petersburg, Russia, you would be taken away by its sheer size and extremely lavish décor. Room after room is embellished with exotic marble, rare woods, elaborate mosaics, and extravagant gold.

One room in this fortress is totally dedicated to a stunning assortment of armor. It was started by Emperor Alexander I and was added to by many Russian emperors over the years. Today this collection contains more than 15,000 pieces of weaponry.

As believers, we have been given powerful spiritual weapons. The apostle Paul refers to these as the "whole armor of God," and it is designed to cover us from head to toe and protect us when we go to war against the enemy. We have everything we need to stand against the enemy and achieve victory through Jesus Christ.

The emphasis of this lesson:

Under the inspiration of the Holy Spirit, Paul instructs us to put on the whole armor of God. When we receive the divine power of the Holy Spirit, that power begins to dress us in God's armor. Included in this weaponry is the loinbelt of truth, breastplate of righteousness, shoes of peace, shield of faith, helmet of salvation, sword of the Spirit, and lance of prayer.

An Urgent Message From Paul To the Ephesian Believers and Us

In our first lesson, we focused on Paul's message to the church of Ephesus in which he said, "Finally, my brethren, be strong in the Lord, and in the power of his might" (Ephesians 6:10). We saw that the word "finally" in Greek means *for the rest of the matter*, and it was a word used in secular documents to prepare the reader for the most important point which had been saved to the very end.

When Paul wrote to the Ephesian believers, they were struggling in their everyday living. A careful reading of Ephesians 4 reveals that they were experiencing problems in their relationships. These included gossiping, backbiting, anger, malice, and bitterness. Their words and actions did not reflect those of victorious people of faith. Although their heads were filled with a great deal of spiritual knowledge, their behavior was much like the world.

That is why Paul wrote to them and basically said, "Finally, brethren, if you don't remember anything else I've said in this letter, please remember this, because I saved the most important thing to the very end. Be strong in the Lord and in the power of His might."

The word "brethren" here is a translation of the Greek word *adelphos*, which in a military sense describes *a fellow fighter* or *comrade in battle*. Like Alexander the Great said of his soldiers, Paul said of his Christian comrades, "We are brothers in battle, and I'm proud to fight alongside you."

We Are Commanded To 'Be Strong in the Lord'

He then commanded them — *and us* — to "be strong in the Lord." We saw that the word "strong" in Greek is the word *endunamoo*. It is a compound of the Greek word *en*, which means *to place something into a container like water into a vessel*; and the word *dunamis*, which is the word for *power*. It is the word used to describe *the invading force of an army* and the very word that Jesus used in Acts 1:8 to describe the supernatural power of the Holy Spirit that fills believers. This word *dunamis* also depicts the powerful force of nature, which means when the power of the Holy Spirit shows up, it is like a spiritual hurricane, tornado, or an earthquake that shakes things up. When His power arrives on the scene, it is like all of Heaven's army is poised and in position to drive back the forces of evil.

When the words *en* and *dunamis* are compounded in Ephesians 6:10 to form the word *endunamoo*, it pictures *the power of a whole army being deposited into a person*. It is *inner strengthening* or *supernatural enablement*. It is a picture of *explosive, superhuman power that comes with enormous energy and produces phenomenal, extraordinary, and unparalleled results being deposited into a receptacle*. God Himself has created this divine *dunamis* power, not to be a free-floating energy that just drifts in the universe, but to be placed into — *en* — a receptacle, into a container, into a vessel. And that is where we enter the picture. God fashioned us to be the receptacles and containers of this divine power.

The word *endunamoo* — translated as "strong" in Ephesians 6:10 — was used by classical Greek writers to describe individuals who had been touched with power from the gods to perform extra-special, superhuman tasks. Once they were touched, it suddenly transformed them into superhuman beings that had strength and abilities they didn't have before.

Paul specifically chose this word *endunamoo* to describe what happens to us when we are touched by the supernatural power of the Holy Spirit. It doesn't matter how weak we were before; His power transforms us and provides us with superhuman abilities. The power God graces us with turns mere men into champions who possess superhuman, supernatural strength.

Even the Greek tense used in this verse is important. The phrase "be strong" is in the present passive imperative tense, which means this is not simply a suggestion to receive this power; it is a *command.* In the strongest of words, Paul was telling the Ephesians — *and us* — to receive the infusion of God's supernatural power as soon as possible. It is exactly what is needed to transform us and give us the supernatural abilities necessary to be dressed and function in the spiritual weaponry He has provided us.

What Does It Mean To 'Put On' God's Armor?

In Ephesians 6:11, Paul goes on to say, "Put on the whole armour of God, that ye may be able to stand against the wiles of the devil." What's very unique about this verse is that the words "put on" are a translation of the exact same word for "power" in verse 10 — the Greek word *enduo,* a compound of the word *en* and the word *dunamis.* The word *en* means *into*, such as in placing water into a vessel, and the word *dunamis* describes *divine power*, like the force of nature. The word *dunamis* also depicts *the forces of an entire army*. When the words *en* and *dunamis* are compounded to form *enduo*, it pictures *the power of a whole army being deposited into a person, providing superhuman power that comes with enormous energy and produces phenomenal, extraordinary, and unparalleled results being deposited into a receptacle.*

Now, when many believers read "Put on the whole armour of God," they immediately think they need to dress themselves in this weaponry. Some Christians go so far as to get up every morning and go through the motions of verbally and symbolically putting on each piece of spiritual weaponry. They say things like, "I buckle on my belt of truth and put on my breastplate of righteousness. I strap on my shoes of peace and raise up my shield of faith. I place my helmet of salvation on my head, secure the lance of prayer to my belt, and grab the sword of the Spirit in my right hand." If you are doing this and it helps you in your faith, that's great. But please realize that going through these motions doesn't actually put God's armor on you.

When you receive the divine power of the Holy Spirit, the Spirit of God begins to dress you. That is the inherent meaning of the word *enduo*, which is translated here as "put on." When God's power hits you, it buckles the belt of truth around your waist and puts the breastplate of righteousness across your chest. It straps on your shoes of peace and raises your shield of faith. Likewise, it is God's power that places the helmet of salvation on your head, secures the lance of prayer to your belt, and places the sword of the Spirit in your hand.

In other words, as long as you walk in the power of God, that power will dress you in spiritual weaponry to live your life in victory. So, the way for you to be dressed in the whole armor of God — or to "put on" spiritual weaponry — is to receive God's divine infusion of power, which Paul describes in verse 10.

The 'Whole Armor' of God

You may be thinking, *What does the Bible mean when it says the "whole armor" of God?* The phrase "whole armour" in Greek is the word *panoplia*, which pictures *a soldier fully dressed in his armor from head to toe*. It is *the full attire and weaponry of a soldier*, which primarily included seven pieces of armor. Though not all-inclusive, the following hardware was required for a soldier to be fully dressed for battle: the loinbelt, breastplate, shoes, shield, helmet, sword, and lance.

Keep in mind that when Paul wrote what we have come to know as the book of Ephesians, he had been imprisoned numerous times, and had therefore been around many Roman soldiers. He had seen firsthand the weaponry and dress of these warriors. So when he wrote Ephesians 6:11 and said, "Put on the whole armour of God…," he was referring to the armor of a fully dressed Roman soldier.

The Loinbelt of Truth

The first piece of armor Paul mentioned is the *loinbelt of truth*, which represents God's Word. All Roman soldiers wore a loinbelt. If you were to describe the clothing a man was wearing, you would probably mention his shirt, his pants, his shoes, and his jacket if he had one. His belt would be low on the list or not make the list at all.

Although the loinbelt was the least impressive and most commonplace piece of weaponry that the Roman soldier wore, it was the central piece of armor that held all the other parts together. For instance, the loinbelt wrapped around the breastplate and held it in place. The shield rested on a clip on one side of the loinbelt, and on the other side was another clip on which the Roman soldier hung his massive sword when it wasn't in use. Furthermore, on the back of the loinbelt was a pouch that contained lances that a soldier used to attack his enemy from a distance

Make no mistake: the loinbelt was more than just a decorative item. If the Roman soldier did not have his loinbelt on, he would literally be in pieces. Not only did it hold all the other pieces of armor in place, it also had long straps that protected the reproductive organs. If a man was hit in his loins and he was unprotected, he would lose his ability to reproduce. This is very important as we will see in upcoming lessons.

The Breastplate of Righteousness

Of all the pieces of weaponry, the breastplate was the heaviest piece of equipment that the Roman soldier owned. It covered the front and the back of the soldier and was often referred to as a "coat of mail." This piece of weaponry began at the bottom of the neck and extended down past the waist to the knees. From the waist to the knees, it took on the resemblance of a skirt.

Because it protected all the vital organs, the breastplate was considered a defensive piece of armor. At the same time, it was also considered an offensive weapon because of its brilliance. As soldiers marched together side-by-side, the brightness of the midday sun would shine on each breastplate and create a blinding glare in the eyes of the enemy.

In a similar way, the righteousness that God has given us is the most brilliant and glorious piece of our weaponry. As we march in the "Son-light" of Jesus, we reflect the power of His radiance into the face of our enemy. Likewise, the *breastplate of righteousness* also protects our vital organs — which includes our heart.

Shoes of Peace

The third piece of armor Paul named is the *shoes of peace*. The Roman soldier's shoes were not like the Roman sandals that people wear today, which are merely a flimsy little piece of twine wrapped around the heel and the toe. These shoes were what we might call *killer shoes*, and they were made of two distinct pieces.

The first piece of the Roman shoe was called a greave, and it was a piece of bronze or brass that was wrapped around the soldier's lower leg. Beginning right at the top of the knee, it extended down past the calf of the leg and rested on top of the foot. Because these tube-like pieces of metal covered the lower legs of the soldier, the Roman soldier's shoes looked like boots that were made of brass! These greaves protected the soldier's legs as he marched through rocky and thorny places.

The second part of the Roman soldier's shoe was the thick, leather bottom that was strapped tightly around his foot. Affixed on the underside of each shoe were extremely dangerous spikes called hobnails. These one-to two-inch long hobnails were used to hold a Roman soldier firmly in place when he was in battle. When he put his feet onto the ground, he was firmly planted and very difficult to move.

In the same way, when we wear our spiritual shoes, God's peace holds us firmly in place. When the enemy tries to push us out of our position, the peace of God grounds us in Christ so that we become very difficult to move. And the greaves of our shoes protect us from being beat up or cut up when we have to trudge through thorny situations and rocky places.

The Shield of Faith

The Roman soldier's shield was simply massive. It was made of multiple layers of animal hide that were tightly woven together and then framed along the edges by a strong piece of metal or wood. It was both tall and wide and was about the size of a small door. When a man came into the Roman infantry, he was measured, and a customized shield was made for his own specifications to make sure he was covered from the top to the bottom and from side to side.

As a believer, when you become a soldier in God's army, you receive a *shield of faith*. The Bible says, "...God has dealt to each one a measure of faith" (Romans 12:3 *NKJV*). That means you don't have to worry about having the same amount of faith as anyone else. You have all the faith you need and are completely covered from head to foot.

The Helmet of Salvation

Roman soldiers also wore a special helmet. It was made out of metal, and it completely covered the sides and the front of the face as well as the back of the head down to the neck. If a soldier had on his helmet, his head would be protected from being severed by the enemy's battle ax. Similarly, we find that God has given us a *helmet of salvation* to protect our mind and keep our head on straight.

On the top of the soldier's helmet was a brightly-colored plume of horse-hair. This made a soldier extremely noticeable. Even from quite a distance away, the fountain of horsehair affixed to the helmet quickly revealed the identity of who was in front of you.

The fact is, your salvation is the most noticeable thing God has done in your life. When you meet a person who is saved, you notice it almost immediately. There is just something very different about him or her. You can hear it in the way that person talks and see it in how he or she lives. Indeed, salvation is noticeable.

The Sword of the Spirit

The next piece of weaponry Paul mentioned is the *sword of the Spirit.* Although there were many kinds of swords used during this time in history, the sword the Roman soldier carried was double-edged, about 19 inches long, and designed to fight the enemy in close combat. This deadly weapon was used to jab, stab, and totally massacre an enemy.

Our sword is called the sword of the Spirit, which is the Word of God. This means the Word of God in our mouth has lethal stabbing power. It has the ability to put the enemy on the run and to render him inoperative. That is the power of God's Word coming out of our mouth.

The Lance of Prayer

The last piece of weaponry Paul named is one that is sometimes overlooked. It is the equivalent of the Roman soldier's lance, and we call it the *lance of prayer.* It is mentioned in Ephesians 6:18, which says, "Praying always with all prayer and supplication in the Spirit…."

Soldiers would use a lance to hurl at an enemy while they were still at a distance. In many ways, prayer is a lot like a lance. When used effectively, prayer can become like a spear we hurl at the devil and his demonic forces to keep them from getting close to us. This is the power of prayer and intercession.

These seven pieces of weaponry make up the whole armor of God. Paul said we are to "Put on the whole armour of God that ye may be able to stand against the wiles of the devil" (Ephesians 6:11). The words "to stand" are the word *stenai* in Greek, which means *to stand upright.* It is the picture of a Roman soldier who is standing tall and upright with his shoulders thrown back and his head lifted high. He is a proud and confident soldier, not one who is slumped over in defeat and despondency.

When you receive the infusion of God's power, you are dressed in spiritual armor, and that armor puts you in a winning position! In our next lesson, we will pull back the curtain and take an up-close look at our enemy — the devil. Who is he? And what does he do?

STUDY QUESTIONS

Study to shew thyself approved unto God, a workman that needeth not to be ashamed, rightly dividing the word of truth.
— 2 Timothy 2:15

1. Take a moment to list all seven pieces of the armor of God. Which piece is most intriguing to you? Why?
2. Prior to this lesson, what did you think the Bible meant when it says, "Put on the whole armor of God?
3. How has this teaching changed your understanding of being dressed in God's armor?

PRACTICAL APPLICATION

But be ye doers of the word, and not hearers only, deceiving your own selves.
— James 1:22

1. If the Roman soldier did not have his loinbelt on, he would literally be in pieces. It was the one part of armor that held everything else in place. What does this tell you about the vital importance of the loinbelt of truth (God's Word) in your life?
2. When you receive the divine power of the Holy Spirit, the Spirit of God begins to dress you. Being arrayed in God's spiritual weaponry is not a result of your human efforts. It is the result of surrendering yourself to God and abiding in relationship with Him. What practical steps can you take to surrender yourself to Him daily and invest personal time in His presence?

LESSON 3

TOPIC

The Devil, Who He Is and What He Does

SCRIPTURES

1. **Ephesians 6:11** — Put on the whole armour of God, that ye may be able to stand against the wiles of the devil.
2. **Revelation 9:11** — And they had a king over them, which is the angel of the bottomless pit, whose name in the Hebrew tongue is Abaddon, but in the Greek tongue hath his name Apollyon.
3. **Revelation 12:10** — ...For the accuser of our brethren is cast down, which accused them before our God day and night.
4. **1 Peter 5:8** — Be sober, be vigilant; because your adversary the devil, as a roaring lion, walketh about, seeking whom he may devour.
5. **2 Corinthians 11:14** — And no marvel; for Satan himself is transformed into an angel of light.
6. **Luke 11:19** — And if I by Beelzebub cast out devils, by whom do your sons cast them out?
7. **Revelation 12:9** — And the great dragon was cast out, that old serpent, called the Devil, and Satan...
8. **Matthew 6:13** — And lead us not into temptation, but deliver us from evil.
9. **John 8:44** — Ye are of your father the devil...he was a murderer from the beginning...
10. **Matthew 9:34** — ...the prince of the devils [demons].
11. **Ephesians 2:2** — ...the prince of the power of the air...
12. **John 14:30** — ...the prince of this world cometh, and hath nothing in me.
13. **Colossians 2:15** (*AMPC*) — [God] disarmed the principalities and powers that were ranged against us and made a bold display and public example of them, in triumphing over them in Him [Jesus] and in it [the cross].

GREEK WORDS

1. "accuser" — **κατήγορος** (*kategoros*): compound of *kata* and *agora*; to publicly accuse in the marketplace; accuser; prosecutor
2. "adversary" — **ἀντίδικος** (*antidikos*): used for a lawyer who argued in a court of law; pictures a prosecuting attorney who argues against the accused; an accuser who attempts to bring a guilty charge to a person on the basis of information from past actions or deeds; an active opponent
3. "devil" — **διάβολος** (*diabolos*): one who repetitiously strikes until successfully penetrating an object in order to ruin it, affect it, or take it captive; to slander, accuse, or defame; to penetrate by continuous assault; to ensnare with a net
4. "prince" — **ἄρχοντι** (*archonti*): prince or chief; one who holds the first place or one who holds the highest rank or seat of power
5. "serpent" — **ὄφις** (*ophis*): and it simply describes a snake of any type; it is also used to denote cunningness or cleverness

SYNOPSIS

Why do nations have weapons? Why would a Russian Emperor like Alexander I and the emperors who followed him amass a collection of more than 15,000 pieces of weaponry? The answer is simple: they had enemies.

The same is true for us spiritually. We have an enemy. He hates the Gospel, detests the Church, and works around the clock to discredit the message of Jesus Christ. Rather than hide from this invisible foe, we must turn to the Scriptures and see what God has to say about him.

There are many names, symbols, and types for the devil throughout the Old and New Testaments, each revealing a different facet of his twisted, perverted nature and his mode of operation. By understanding who he is and what he does, we can learn how to use our God-given weapons to escape his snares and walk in victory.

The emphasis of this lesson:

Throughout the Old and New Testaments, there are many names, symbols, and types for the devil, each revealing a different facet of the devil's

twisted, perverted nature and his mode of operation. This lesson will cover 17 titles assigned to him.

The Full Force of Heaven's Army Is Available to You!

Our anchor verse for this series is Ephesians 6:11, which says, "Put on the whole armour of God, that ye may be able to stand against the wiles of the devil." In our last lesson, we learned that the words "put on" are a translation of the Greek word *enduo*, which is a compound of the word *en* and the word *dunamis*. The word *en* means *into*, such as putting water into a container or vessel, and the word *dunamis* is the Greek word for *power*.

Dunamis is the very word Jesus used to describe the *power* of the Holy Spirit in Acts 1:8 when He said, "But ye shall receive power, after that the Holy Ghost is come upon you...." It is also the word Paul used to describe the *power* of the gospel in Romans 1:16 when he said, "For I am not ashamed of the gospel of Christ: for it is the power of God unto salvation...."

This word *dunamis* describes *phenomenal supernatural energy*. It is the very word to describe *a force of nature* like a tornado, a hurricane, or an earthquake. And it is the same word used to describe *the full might of an advancing army*. Thus, the power of the Gospel when it is preached and the power of the Holy Spirit when He moves are like a divine hurricane, tornado, or earthquake that really shakes up the powers of darkness and changes society. When the Gospel is preached and the power of the Holy Spirit arrives on the scene, it is like an invasion of Heaven's army.

When we come to Ephesians 6:10, the word *dunamis* and the word *en* are compounded to form the word *enduo*. This pictures *the power of a whole army being deposited into a person*. It is *inner strengthening* or *supernatural enablement*. It is a picture of *explosive, superhuman power that comes with enormous energy and produces phenomenal, extraordinary, and unparalleled results being deposited into a receptacle*. God Himself has created this *dunamis* power, not to be a free-floating energy that just drifts in the universe, but to be placed into (*en*) a receptacle or a container.

That is us — we are the receptacle. God fashioned us to be the containers of this divine power, which is *in the Lord*. Since we are in Christ, we are rubbing elbows with this power all the time. Although we may not always be mentally aware of it, the very fact that both we and this special power are locked up *in the Lord* means we are never far away from a fresh surge of superhuman power into our own human spirits. We just have to take it by faith. God could not have made this any simpler for us.

Seventeen Names That Depict the Devil in Scripture

Again, the reason God has given us spiritual armor is so that we "...may be able to stand against the wiles of the devil" (Ephesians 6:10). The Bible uses 17 names throughout the Old and New Testament to describe the devil and the way he operates. These include:

1. Abaddon (Revelation 9:11)
2. Accuser (Revelation 12:10)
3. Adversary (1 Peter 5:8)
4. Angel of light (2 Corinthians 11:14)
5. Apollyon (Revelation 9:11)
6. Beelzebub (Matthew 10:25; 12:24)
7. Belial (2 Corinthians 6:15)
8. Devil (Ephesians 6:11; 1 Peter 5:8; Revelation 12:9)
9. Dragon (Revelation 12:9)
10. Evil one (Matthew 6:13)
11. Murderer (John 8:44)
12. Prince of this world (John 12:31)
13. Prince of demons (Matthew 9:34 *NIV*)
14. Prince of the power of the air (Ephesians 2:2)
15. Roaring lion (1 Peter 5:8)
16. Satan (Luke 10:18)
17. Serpent (Revelation 12:9)

These are names, symbols, and types of Satan. Let's take a look at each of these names and an example of where they are found in Scripture.

Abaddon and Apollyon

Of the 17 names, symbols, and types for Satan, two are devoted to his insatiable desire to *destroy*. The names *Abaddon* and *Apollyon* are used to describe the devil in Revelation 9:11:

> **And they had a king over them, which is the angel of the bottomless pit, whose name in the Hebrew tongue is Abaddon, but in the Greek tongue hath his name Apollyon.**

The name *Abaddon* is the Hebrew equivalent of the Greek name *Apollyon*, but both of these names mean *destroyer*. Destruction is in the devil's very nature. You can be certain that demon spirits, over which Satan rules as a king, possess the same destructive nature as their master. They also operate according to the instructions Satan gives them as he sends them forth to *destroy*.

Accuser

In Revelation 12:10, the devil is called the *accuser*. The Bible says:

> **...For the accuser of our brethren is cast down, which accused them before our God day and night.**

The word "accuser" is the Greek word *kategoros*. It is a compound of the word *kata*, meaning *down*, and the word *agora*, which is the word for the *marketplace*. When these words are compounded, it means *to publicly accuse someone in the marketplace in order to take them down*. It depicts *an accuser* or *prosecutor*. The devil feeds on publicly slandering and accusing people, and the information in the mass media confirms this.

Adversary

Another title for the devil is *adversary*, and we find this mentioned in First Peter 5:8:

> **Be sober, be vigilant; because your adversary the devil, as a roaring lion, walketh about, seeking whom he may devour.**

The word "adversary" in Greek is *antidikos*, which is a compound of the word *anti*, meaning *against*, and a form of the word *diko*, meaning *righteousness*. Thus, when the Bible calls the devil the *adversary*, it is saying that he is totally opposed to righteousness and anything that is good, just, and fair.

Furthermore, the word *antidikos* (adversary) is also the word used for *a lawyer who argued in a court of law*. This word pictures *a prosecuting attorney who argues against the accused; an accuser who attempts to bring a guilty charge to a person on the basis of information from past actions or deeds*. That is exactly what the devil does and why we need to claim God's forgiveness and cleansing through the blood of Jesus!

Angel of Light

Satan is also called an *angel of light*, which means he disguises himself and masquerades as something that he is not. We find this title is assigned to him in Second Corinthians 11:14:

> **And no marvel; for Satan himself is transformed into an angel of light.**

In this verse, the apostle Paul is talking about the problematic activities of false prophets, false teachers, false apostles, and deceivers who were trying to worm their way into the Corinthian church. Like Satan, these imposters were twisting the truth in order to project an image of something that was not true.

Beelzebub

Another name given to the devil is *Beelzebub*. Jesus actually cited this name in Luke 11:19:

> **And if I by Beelzebub cast out devils, by whom do your sons cast them out?**

The name *Beelzebub* first appeared in the Old Testament and was initially used by the Philistines to describe the god of Ekron, and it literally meant *lord of the flies* (*see* 2 Kings 1:2-6).

Originally it was spelled "Baalzebub," but as time progressed, the Jews altered *Baalzebub* to *Beelzebub*, which added an even dimmer idea to this particular name of the devil. This new name "Beelzebub" thus came to mean *lord of the dunghill* or *lord of the manure.*

Two powerful and important images of Satan are presented in these two names. First, he is presented as "Baalzebub," the *lord of the flies*. This pictures Satan masquerading himself as the lord of demon spirits. Obviously, the Philistines looked upon demon spirits in the same way one would look upon nasty, dirty *flies* that bite, torment, and irritate.

Secondly, Satan is presented as "Beelzebub," the *lord of the dunghill.* By adding a twist to this particular name, the Jews revealed a very important characteristic of the devil. Just like nasty, dirty flies, both the devil and his evil spirits are attracted to "dunghills," or environments where rotting, stinking carnality pervades. This is the environment where Satan thrives best.

Belial

The devil is also assigned the name *Belial*, which is of Greek origination and means *worthless*. This title is always used in connection with *filthiness* and *wickedness*. Whenever it is used, either in the Old Testament or the New Testament, it is used to depict extremely evil men. Take Eli's sons, for example. First Samuel 2:12 says:

> **Now the sons of Eli were sons of Belial; they knew not the Lord.**

What an example Eli's sons were of this word *Belial*. They were fornicators and thieves, full of idolatry and rebellion. These terrible traits were ingrained into their character to such an extent that God's judgment came upon them, and they were removed from the scene in one day's time. Because First Samuel 2:12 calls them "sons of *Belial*," we know they obtained this horrid behavior from Satan, who is himself the origination of the name *Belial*.

Devil

Of course, Satan is also called the *devil*. We see this name mentioned 40 times in the New Testament alone, including its appearance in our anchor verse Ephesians 6:11:

> **Put on the whole armour of God, that ye may be able to stand against the wiles of the devil.**

The word "devil" is the Greek word *diabolos*, and it depicts *one who repetitiously strikes until successfully penetrating an object in order to ruin it, affect it, or take it captive*. It is the very word that means *to slander, accuse, or defame*. It carries the idea of *penetration by continuous assault* or *to ensnare with a net*.

Therefore, in the name "devil," we are not only given the proper name of our archenemy but also his mode of operation. His name means that he is *one who continually strikes and strikes and strikes again* — beating against the walls of people's minds over and over again — until, finally, he breaks through and penetrates their thought processes.

Dragon

The word *dragon* is also used to depict the devil. No verse captures this better than Revelation 12:9:

> **And the great dragon was cast out, that old serpent, called the Devil, and Satan, which deceiveth the whole world....**

The terms "dragon" and "serpent" are the same word in Greek — the word *ophis*. It is clear from this verse that these terms are used interchangeably in reference to Satan's twisted, demented, and perverted nature. By employing both of these images, the Bible presents the devil as a deadly, poisonous, ready-to-strike-and-kill creature.

Evil One

The next name assigned to the devil in the Bible is the *evil one*, and it can be found in what is traditionally called "The Lord's Prayer." In Matthew 6:13, the Lord Jesus gave His disciples an example of how to pray, saying:

> **And lead us not into temptation, but deliver us from evil....**

What's interesting about this verse is that in the Greek language, the text more accurately reads, "...but deliver us from *the* evil one." From this usage, we know that Jesus looked on the devil as the "evil one." No one was more familiar with Satan than Jesus. Hence, it is important to us that Jesus, knowing the devil so well, would label him like this.

Murderer

In His confrontation with the Pharisees, the Lord Jesus told us that the devil is a *murderer*. We see this in John 8:44:

> **Ye are of your father the devil...he was a murderer from the beginning....**

The murderous nature of Satan first manifested in Genesis 4:8, when he inspired Cain to slay his brother Abel. It was also Satan's murderous nature that inspired King Herod to kill all the babies in Bethlehem. We continue to see the devil's murderous nature in the deaths of millions of Early Christian martyrs and still today wherever murderous injustice prevails on the earth. Specifically, we see his murderous nature in the abortion of millions of babies all over the world today. Murder is a part of Satan's demented nature.

The Prince of Demons

Another name given to the devil is the *prince of demons*. We see this designation in Matthew 9:34:

> **But the Pharisees said, He casteth out devils through the prince of the devils [demons].**

The word "prince" in this verse is the Greek word *archonti*, which means *prince or chief*; *one who holds the first place* or *one who holds the highest rank or seat of power*. The title *prince of demons* most assuredly reveals that Satan holds the highest-ranking seat among a host of diabolical spirits. The word "prince" denotes that there is rank and file and some form of organization to Satan's system of governing his kingdom.

The Prince of the Power of the Air

In addition to being called the *prince of demons*, the devil is also referred to by the apostle Paul as the *prince of the power of the air*. We read this in Ephesians 2:2:

> **Wherein in time past ye walked according to the course of this world, according to the prince of the power of the air, the spirit that now worketh in the children of disobedience.**

This verse is in agreement with Ephesians 6:12, which states that under Satan's control there are varying degrees of spiritually wicked power. These include: principalities, powers, rulers of the darkness of this world, and spiritual wickedness in high places. As the *prince of the power of the air*, Satan is at the very top of all these powers.

The Prince of This World

Interestingly, just before going to the Cross, Jesus called Satan the *prince of this world*. We see this in John 14:30:

> **Hereafter I will not talk much with you: for the prince of this world cometh, and hath nothing in me.**

By calling Satan the *prince of this world*, Jesus recognized Satan's temporal control over certain things in this earthly sphere. The word "world" here is the Greek word *kosmos*, which describes *the systems of the world*, such as education, entertainment, and business. This is what Satan is the "prince" over — where he holds *the chief seat of power*.

You might remember that Satan himself personally offered Jesus the "kingdoms of this world" during Jesus' 40 days and nights of testing in the wilderness (*see* Luke 4:5-7). Jesus was confronted by the *prince of this world* during those 40 days and resisted the devil's power until His adversary fled. Jesus spoke from personal experience when he referred to this temporal claim of Satan.

A Roaring Lion

One of the most familiar titles assigned to Satan is *a roaring lion*, which is found in First Peter 5:8:

> **Be sober, be vigilant; because your adversary the devil, as a roaring lion, walketh about, seeking whom he may devour.**

What awe and fear the mighty roar of a lion strikes in the heart of frail men! But Peter said the devil is *like* "a roaring lion." This means, in the case of the devil, his roar is more fearsome than his bite. According to the apostle Paul, Satan has no teeth. Look at what he declares in Colossians 2:15 (*AMPC*):

> **[God] disarmed the principalities and powers that were ranged against us and made a bold display and public example of them, in triumphing over them in Him [Jesus] and in it [the cross].**

By means of the Cross and the resurrection, Jesus Christ stripped all demonic powers bare of the authority they once possessed. Jesus' victory over them was so thorough that He even "made a bold display and public example of them."

However, this has not stopped the devil from trying to *sound* dreadful. Through his continuous hassling of our thoughts, his insinuations about failure, his concoction of unrealistic fears in our souls, and his constant onslaught against our minds, Satan tries to beat us down into defeat. This constant "roaring" in our souls is just another attempt of the adversary to wear us down, wear us out, and then swallow us up in self-pity.

Notice that the object of the adversary is to seek those "...whom he may devour" (1 Peter 5:8). Satan is not seeking just *anyone* to devour; he is seeking those whom he *may* devour. In other words, the enemy is looking for those who are *weak in faith*, *ignorant of the Word of God*, *isolated unto themselves*, and *not mature enough* to stand in the face of his constant, hassling allegations. These are the individuals this "roaring lion" is seeking after, and his object is to *devour* them.

Satan

Of course, the name *Satan* is probably the most recognized and widely used titles for the devil. We see this name throughout the Scriptures, including Revelation 12:9:

> **And the great dragon was cast out, that old serpent, called the Devil, and Satan, which deceiveth the whole world....**

This enemy of both God and man is called "Satan," which is taken from the Hebrew word *shatana* and means *to hate and to accuse*. It is used more than 50 times in the Old and New Testament, and it also carries with it the ideas of *slander and false accusation*.

Serpent

The last name given to the devil is also found in Revelation 12:9. It is *that old serpent*. This word "serpent" is the Greek word *ophis*, and it simply describes *a snake of any type*. It is also used to denote *cunningness* or *cleverness*. Indeed, the devil is as deadly and poisonous as a venomous snake ready to strike and kill, and he has been in position to do so since the very beginning of time.

These are the 17 names that are used throughout the Bible to describe the devil and his mode of operation. He is a real, supernatural enemy that should be taken seriously. That is why we are instructed to "Put on the whole armour of God, that ye may be able to stand against the wiles of the devil" (Ephesians 6:11).

In our next lesson, we will take a closer look at what the "wiles" and "devices" of the devil are.

STUDY QUESTIONS

Study to shew thyself approved unto God, a workman that needeth not to be ashamed, rightly dividing the word of truth.
— 2 Timothy 2:15

1. Out of the 17 names that depict the devil in Scripture, which ones were you not aware of? Which titles were most surprising? Which were most grievous? Why?
2. Which name (or names) best describes the way Satan attacks you and your family most often? What methods does he use when he comes against you?
3. Although Satan is a formidable foe that we should take seriously, we must also always remember that God is greater, and that in Christ we are triumphant. Take time to reflect on these passages and identify what God says about your position of victory in Him:
   - Romans 16:20
   - 1 John 4:4
   - Luke 10:19
   - Colossians 2:15
   - 2 Corinthians 2:14

PRACTICAL APPLICATION

But be ye doers of the word, and not hearers only, deceiving your own selves.
—James 1:22

1. The devil is looking for individuals who are *weak in faith*, *ignorant of the Word of God*, and *isolated unto themselves*. These are those "…whom he may devour" (1 Peter 5:8). Does this describe you? If so, run to God now! Dive deep into His Word! And begin connecting with others who are passionately pursuing Him with their whole heart!
2. If you will yield yourself to God — daily surrendering all that you are to Him — and ask Him to empower you with His *dunamis* power, He will strengthen you against the enemy's attacks and do in you what He declared through the prophet Habakkuk. Meditate on this amazing promise and allow the Holy Spirit to accomplish this creative miracle in you.

   The Lord God is my Strength, my personal bravery, and my invincible army; He makes my feet like hinds' feet and will make me to walk [not stand still in terror, but to walk]

and make [spiritual] progress upon my high places [of trouble, suffering, or responsibility]!

Habakkuk 3:19 (*AMPC*)

LESSON 4

TOPIC

The Wiles, Devices, and Deception of the Devil

SCRIPTURES

1. **Ephesians 6:11** — Put on the whole armour of God, that ye may be able to stand against the wiles of the devil.
2. **2 Corinthians 2:11** — …we are not ignorant of his [Satan's] devices.
3. **2 Corinthians 10:5** — Casting down imaginations, and every high thing that exalteth itself against the knowledge of God, and bringing into captivity every thought to the obedience of Christ.

GREEK WORDS

1. "whole armour" — **πανοπλία** (*panoplia*): pictures a soldier fully dressed in his armor from head to toe; the full attire and weaponry of a soldier; though not all-inclusive, the following hardware was required for a soldier to be fully dressed for battle: the loinbelt, breastplate, shoes, shield, helmet, sword, and lance
2. "to stand" — **στῆναι** (*stenai*): to stand upright
3. "against" — **πρός** (*pros*): against; denotes a forward position or a face-to-face encounter
4. "wiles" — **μεθοδεία** (*methodeia*): with a road; to operate on an avenue; to operate on a chart or route; no happenstance, as this portrays direction and objective; direction or strategy; conveys craftiness and deceit; where we get the word method
5. "devices" — **νοήματα** (*noemata*): describes a mind that is scheming, calculating, conniving, devious, shrewd, sly, or clever; denotes the

insidious and malevolent plot of Satan to fill the human mind with confusion; carries the idea of a deceived mind

6. "devil" — **διάβολος** (*diabolos*): one who repetitiously strikes until successfully penetrating an object in order to ruin it, affect it, or take it captive; to slander, accuse, or defame; to penetrate by continuous assault; to ensnare with a net

SYNOPSIS

The fact that we have real enemies in this world means we have to have real weapons — weapons that are powerfully effective. Alexander I, the emperor of Russia, was well aware of this fact, which is why he armed himself and his country with great weapons. He even started a collection of armor, which was added to by his successors and contains more than 15,000 magnificent pieces.

As Christians, we have a formidable enemy of our faith. The Bible identifies him as the old serpent, the roaring lion, the accuser of the brethren, and Satan. To effectively defeat our foe and the hordes of hell that do his bidding, we must dress in our spiritual armor and understand how Satan operates. With this divine knowledge and the empowerment of the Holy Spirit, we can move from being a victim to being a victor in Jesus Christ!

The emphasis of this lesson:

The devil has a one-track plan of attack against your mind. Through cunning and calculating strategies, he dangles his deceptions in front of you, hoping you'll take the bait. Again and again he strikes and strikes against your mind and emotions, with the ultimate goal of penetrating your thinking and taking you captive to do his will. Understanding how the devil operates will enable you to dismantle his attacks and live victoriously.

Suit Up in God's Armor and Stand Against the Enemy

In Ephesians 6:11, Paul wrote, "Put on the whole armour of God that ye may be able to stand against the wiles of the devil." Thus far, we have seen that our spiritual armor mirrors the armor of a Roman soldier and consists of seven pieces: the loinbelt of truth, the breastplate of righteousness, the shoes of peace, the shield of faith, the helmet of salvation, the sword of the Spirit, and the lance of prayer and supplication. These are the weapons God has given to the Church, and He commands us to be dressed in them.

What does this spiritual armor enable us to do? The Bible says, "…to stand against the wiles of the devil" (Ephesians 6:11). The words "to stand" are the Greek word *stenai*, which means *to stand upright*. It is the picture of a Roman soldier who is standing upright and tall with his shoulders thrown back and his head lifted high. He is confident — not in himself, but in the mighty weaponry in which he is dressed. Likewise, when you're dressed in the whole armor of God, you can stand confidently against the enemy, knowing you have what you need to defeat the wiles of the devil.

The word "against" in this verse is also important. It is the Greek word *pros*, and it denotes *a forward position* or *a face-to-face encounter*. The use of this word lets us know that at some point in our lives, we are all going to come face to face, eyeball to eyeball, and ribcage to ribcage with the work of the devil. But if we're dressed in the armor of God, we will have the ability to stand confidently — even when we're in close combat with the enemy dealing with his wiles.

What Are the 'Wiles' of the Devil?

In Ephesians 6:11, Paul said that we are to stand against the "wiles of the devil." Understanding this word "wiles" is vital to avoiding the devil's traps. The word "wiles" is the Greek word *methodeia*, which is a compound of the word *meta* and the word *hodas*. The word *meta* means *with*, and the word *hodas* is the Greek word for *a road, an avenue, or a lane*. When you compound these two words together to form *methodeia*, it literally means *with a road*. It depicts *one that is traveling, operating on an avenue*; *one that is operating on a specific chart or route*. There is no happenstance here, as this portrays *direction and objective*; *direction* or *strategy*. This person has a specific goal, and he knows exactly where he is heading. Moreover, the word *methodeia* — translated here as "wiles" — conveys the idea of *craftiness and deceit*. It is from where we get the word *method*.

This is how Satan operates — through "wiles" (*methodeia*). By electing to use this word, Paul tells us how the devil puts his cunning, crafty, subtle, and tricky deception to work. He does not have multiple ways he attacks. He has one main avenue or one road he consistently travels down to attack you. He primarily has only one trick in his bag — and he obviously has learned to use that one trick very well! What is that one trick the devil uses against people? Or perhaps we should more correctly ask, "What is the destination that diabolical road is headed toward?" The answer is found in the meaning of the word "devices."

What Are the Devil's 'Devices'?

The word "devices" is used in Second Corinthians 2:11 to further describe the *wiles* of the devil. Writing under the unction of the Holy Spirit, the apostle Paul said, "Lest Satan should get an advantage of us: for we are not ignorant of his devices."

The word "devices" carries the idea of *mind games*. It is the Greek word *noemata*, and it comes from the word *nous*, which is the word for *the mind* or *the intellect*. However, when the word *nous* becomes *noemata*, it describes *a mind that is scheming, calculating, conniving, devious, shrewd, sly*, or *clever*. It denotes *the insidious and malevolent plot of Satan to fill the human mind with confusion* and carries the idea of *a mind that is scrambled, deceived, and can no longer think correctly*.

Again, the devil has one primary road of attack that he consistently travels — one strategic way of attacking people. That is what the word "wiles" — the Greek word *methodeia* — means. That road is headed toward the *nous*, which is *the mind*. In Second Corinthians 2:11, this word is translated "devices." Satan's objective is to pave a road into your mind and the minds of every human being, and so confuse and scramble it that the mind becomes deceived and can no longer think correctly. This is how "deception" takes root.

How Does 'Deception' Fit Into Satan's Grand Scheme?

When the devil attacks the mind, he often does it through "deception." In Greek, the word "deception" is the word *dolios*, which is a fishing term. It is derived from a word that describes *bait put on a hook to catch fish*. It is the picture of a fish that looks at the bait being dangled in front of him. Although he knows there is a hook in it and that he should avoid it, he becomes hypnotized by continually looking at it, and when he can resist it no longer, he bites the bait and is ensnared by the hook. Thus, this word *dolios* — translated here as "deception" — conveys the idea of *craftiness, cheating, cunning, dishonesty, fraud, guile, and trickery intended to entrap someone in an act of deception*.

The enemy's ultimate goal of deception is that believers will open the door for him to move these lying suggestions from the thought realm into the natural realm, where they become a bona fide reality. A person's belief in a lie will empower the lie — and the devil uses their misdirected faith to make those lies a reality.

When you embrace the devil's mind games — his "devices" — and perceive them as truth, you give power to them! If you do not take charge of your mind and begin to speak God's truth to yourself to combat the devil's lies, the process of deception will continue working in your life. Eventually that process will be complete, and your fears will become reality. When this occurs, you will be deceived in that area of your life.

The Word 'Devil' Is More Than Just a Name

Looking once more at Ephesians 6:11, it says, "Put on the whole armour of God, that ye may be able to stand against the wiles of the devil." In addition to the word "wiles," "devices," and "deception," the meaning of the word "devil" is extremely important. In Greek, it is the word *diabolos*, and it is a compound of the word *dia*, which carries the idea of *penetration*, and the word *balos*, which means *to throw something like a ball or a rock*. When these two words are compounded to form the word *diabolos*, it depicts *one who repetitiously strikes until successfully penetrating an object in order to ruin it, affect it, or take it captive*. Thus, the word devil (*diabolos*) is more than just Satan's name — it is his job description or mode of operation.

Stop and think about how the devil operates. He travels on a road with one lane of attack (*methodeia*) straight to your mind. With *a scheming, calculating, conniving, and devious strategy, he shrewdly* begins to hurl one deceptive thought after another deceptive thought against your mind (*noemata*). He repeatedly strikes and strikes and strikes your mind, hour after hour, day after day, hitting you with lies, suggestions, accusations, and allegations, bombarding you with one slanderous assault after another (*diabolos*). In this way, he lives up to the meaning of his name. Through calculated persistence, the devil attempts to wear you down — looking for an opportunity to make his move and take you captive in one weak moment.

Once a person's mental resistance has been breached, the enemy then strikes with all his fury to penetrate (*dia*) and take captive that person's mind and emotions. If he can find you with your guard down, he will then try to pave a road into your mind (*methodos*) so he can confuse and scramble your mind and emotions with his "mind games" (*noemata*). He baits his hooks, dangling one deception after another in front of you in hopes that you'll bite (*dolios*). His goal is to get you to look at what he is offering long enough so that you'll take the bait and be hooked by his deception. If he succeeds and you begin to believe his lies, your false perceptions will empower his lies to become a reality in your life.

Are you beginning to better understand the sense of urgency behind Paul's command in Ephesians 6:11? If you're ever going to live free from the enemy's tormenting lies and accusations, it is absolutely imperative that you are dressed with the whole armor — the *panoplia* — that comes from God. You need the loinbelt of truth, breastplate of righteousness, shoes (with greaves) of peace, shield of faith, helmet of salvation, sword of the Spirit, and lance of prayer. Only that armor will enable you to stand face-to-face and eyeball-to-eyeball against the devil as he attempts to pave roads into your mind.

Examples of Mental Attacks

One of the best ways to understand how the devil works is by looking at examples of the way he attacks. For instance, the devil may assault your mind by repeatedly telling you that you are a failure. As long as you resist those demonic allegations, they will exert absolutely no power in your life.

But what if you begin to give credence to these lies and to mentally perceive them as the actual truth? Those lies will then begin to control you and dominate your emotions and your thinking. In the end, your faith in those lies will give power to them and will cause them to create a bona fide reality in your life — and you will become a failure.

Many marriages fail because of false allegations that the enemy tries to pound into the mind of each spouse. As long as the couple repels these allegations, the devil's lies exert no power in that marriage. But when one of the spouses begins to pay attention to and dwell on those lies, he or she has taken the first fatal step toward deception.

Take, for instance, the example of a marriage that is in good shape until one of the spouses starts dwelling on unjustified questions and suspicions about the other spouse. This is clearly the work of the enemy to deteriorate the couple's confidence in their marriage. At first, this spouse absolutely knows that these suspicions are outright lies of the devil. Indeed, he or she thinks, *Our marriage has never been better!*

But the enemy continues to pound away on this spouse's mind, and after a period of time, the spouse's mind — battered and weary from worrying — begins to believe those false allegations. That spouse's faith in those lying emotions and suspicions may then empower the lies to become a reality in his or her marriage.

By mentally entertaining these false insinuations, this spouse opens the door for the enemy to penetrate his or her mind. Thus, the process of confusion is implemented; mind games are set in motion; and that believer's perception of things becomes twisted and bent. If this deceiving process is not stopped at this point, it is probably only a matter of time before the weary-minded believer begins to embrace these mental lies as though they were really the truth.

Your Mind Is the Control Center of Your Life

Friend, your mind is the control center of your life. The devil knows this, which is why he targets your thinking and repeatedly attempts to gain access to it. If he can take control of your mind, he can ultimately take control of you. He uses your mind almost like a movie screen, vividly projecting images of what he wants you to believe about yourself, about others, and even about God. He posts pictures of what he wants you to believe and accept about your future, your finances, your marriage, your children, and your health. Why? Because he's trying to get you to bite the bait.

If you listen to his lies and allow them to fester in your mind — if you keep listening and listening to what he says, pondering the possibilities and entertaining all the details again and again — eventually you will begin to believe it as truth. The devil will have successfully paved a road into your mind and your emotions. As you bite the bait about what he is telling you, your faith will empower his lies, and those lies will become your reality.

Your reality will be what you believe. That's why what you listen to and what you believe are so important.

The truth is, the enemy is not the only one after your mind. *God wants your mind too.* That's why He said, "And do not be conformed to this world, but be transformed by the renewing of your mind…" (Romans 12:2 *NKJV*). If you will feed on the Word of God, listening to and believing what He says, your faith will bite the bait of God's Word and will empower His Word to become a reality in your life! That's the way it works.

The more your mind is filled with the Word of God, the more it is renewed with truth. If you renew your mind with what the Bible says about your healing, your marriage, your health, your finances, and your future, your faith will bite the bait about what God says about you, and you will empower that truth to become your reality.

Again, **your reality will be what you believe.**

This is why we're told in Second Corinthians 10:5 that we must "Cast down imaginations, and every high thing that exalts itself against the knowledge of God, and bring into captivity every thought to the obedience of Christ." When the devil tries to fill our minds with vain imaginations, we have to cast them down. We have to shut our ears to the lies and open our ears to the truth. The one we listen to and the one we believe will become our reality.

In our next lesson, we will turn our attention to what the Bible means when it talks about wrestling with principalities and powers.

STUDY QUESTIONS

Study to shew thyself approved unto God, a workman that needeth not to be ashamed, rightly dividing the word of truth.
— 2 Timothy 2:15

1. In your own words, briefly describe the meaning of each of these four key words: *Wiles*; *Devices*; *Deception*; and *Devil.*
2. Using the meanings of these words, explain how they are connected and paint the picture of the way the enemy attacks your mind and emotions.
3. One of the greatest ways to guard against the devil's lies is to *renew your mind* with the truth of God's Word (*see* Romans 12:2). According to Hebrews 4:12 and James 1:21, what can you expect to happen as you humble yourself and spend regular time in the Scriptures? (Also consider Romans 1:16; Psalm 119:9; John 15:3 and 17:17.)

PRACTICAL APPLICATION

But be ye doers of the word, and not hearers only,
deceiving your own selves.
—James 1:22

1. The word "devil" in Greek is *diabolos,* and it depicts *one who repetitiously strikes until successfully penetrating an object in order to ruin it, affect it, or take it captive.* Name one area of your mind and emotions where the enemy has repeatedly been striking and trying to penetrate? How long has this attack been going on?
2. Take a good look at the areas of your thought-life where the devil has repeatedly attacked. What pattern (or patterns) can you observe and learn to guard against moving forward?
3. What is the most successful tactic you've learned to silence the devil's voice when he's bombarding you with his lies?
4. When you embrace the devil's mind games — his "devices" — and perceive them as truth, you give power to them. Get alone with God and pray, *"Lord, have I become a victim of the enemy's devices? If so, what lies am I believing as truth? Is there an area in my life in which I'm deceived? If so, please show me where. In Jesus' name. Amen."*

LESSON 5

TOPIC

Wrestling With Principalities and Powers

SCRIPTURES

1. **Ephesians 6:10-13** — Finally, my brethren, be strong in the Lord, and in the power of his might. Put on the whole armour of God, that ye may be able to stand against the wiles of the devil. For we wrestle not against flesh and blood, but against principalities, against powers, against the rulers of the darkness of this world, against spiritual wickedness in high places. Wherefore take unto you the whole armour of

God, that ye may be able to withstand in the evil day, and having done all, to stand.

GREEK WORDS

1. "wrestle" — **πάλη** (*pale*): struggling, wrestling, or hand-to-hand fighting; also the Greek word from which the Greeks derived the word Palaestra, a famous house of combat sports
2. "against" — **πρός** (*pros*): a close confrontation; a face-to-face encounter
3. "principalities" — **ἀρχάς** (*archas*): used symbolically to denote ancient times; the very beginning or origin; also used to depict individuals who hold the highest and loftiest position of rank and authority; princes or principalities
4. "powers" — **ἐξουσία** (*exousia*): delegated authority; influence; denotes one who has received delegated power; often translated authorities; it could denote those who wielded authority entrusted to them by their superiors
5. "the rulers of the darkness of this world" — **κοσμοκράτωρ** (*kosmokrator*): pictures military training camps where young men were assembled, trained, and turned into a mighty army; the recruits were taught discipline and order, and all that manpower was converted into an organized, disciplined army; a highly trained and aggressive force
6. "spiritual wickedness in high places" — **πονηρία** (*poneria*): destruction, disaster, harm, or danger; malicious or malignant; foul, vile, hostile, and vicious; not only that which is dangerous to the physical body but also to that which is dangerous to the spirit or mind; depicts animals that are savage, wild, vicious, and dangerous

SYNOPSIS

Just as any nation needs to understand its enemy and how it operates, as believers, we need to know our enemy and how he operates. If we are ignorant of our opponent, we are in trouble. But there's no reason for us to be ignorant about the devil because the Bible tells us all about him — even how his demonic troops are marshaled against us. Writing under the inspiration of the Holy Spirit, the apostle Paul gives us a divine blueprint of the strategic hierarchy of Satan's forces, saying,

For we wrestle not against flesh and blood, but against principalities, against powers, against the rulers of the darkness of this world, against spiritual wickedness in high places.
Ephesians 6:12

To successfully stand against Satan and the rulers and powers of darkness at all levels and in all places, God has made sure that we are *dressed to kill*! He has given us powerful, supernatural weapons to effectively keep the devil under our feet where he belongs. And these spiritual weapons are activated as we abide in relationship with Christ.

The emphasis of this lesson:

Paul used the backdrop of the violent sports of the Palaestra to paint a picture of the intensity of our struggle against the devil and his demonic forces. In order to successfully wage war against principalities, powers, rulers of the darkness of this world, and spiritual wickedness in high places, we must be better equipped, alert, and prepared before the fight begins.

A Review of Ephesians 6:10 and 11

In Ephesians 6:10, our anchor verse, the apostle Paul said, "Finally, my brethren, be strong in the Lord, and in the power of his might." In our previous lessons, we have seen that the word "finally" is the equivalent of Paul saying, "Now, to the last and most important matter at hand. I have saved the most important thing for the end of my letter. So, if you don't remember anything else I've said, I want you to remember this and let it stand out in your mind."

Notice Paul addressed them as "my brethren." This word "brethren" is a translation of the Greek word *adelphos*, which is *a term used to describe two or more who were born from the same womb*. It was actually popularized by Alexander the Great, the mighty military leader who used the word to carry the idea of *a comrade* or a *fellow fighter*. Hence, Paul used the word *adelphos* to call the Ephesian believers his *comrades* or *fellow fighters in the faith*.

To all his brothers in battle he said, "Be strong in the Lord." We've seen that this word "strong" in Greek is the word *endunamoo*. It is a compound of the Greek word *en*, which means *to place something into a container or receptacle*, and the word *dunamis*, which is the word for *power*. It describes *the force of nature* — like a hurricane, a tornado, or an earthquake. It also depicts *the full force of an invading army*. Thus, when the power of the Holy Spirit shows up, it is like a spiritual hurricane, tornado, or an earthquake that shakes things up. When His power arrives on the scene, it is like all of Heaven's army is poised and in position to drive back the forces of evil.

It is this amazing *dunamis* power that has been placed into (*en*) some kind of a vessel or a container. In this case, we are the receptacles of this divine power. God fashioned us to hold his power, which means His power is not a free-floating energy that just drifts in the universe. God made this power to be placed *inside* of us. And when it comes in us, it transforms us into superhuman people with supernatural abilities. That's what happens when we receive a fresh touch of God's power.

Knowing the extreme cunningness and calculating ways of the enemy, Paul urged the Ephesian believers — *and us* — to "...Be strong in the Lord, and in the power of his might" (Ephesians 6:10). He then urged us to "Put on the whole armour of God, that ye may be able to stand against the wiles of the devil" (Ephesians 6:11). The phrase "whole armour" is the Greek word *panoplia*, and it pictures *a soldier fully dressed in his armor from head to toe*. For the Roman soldier, this included the loinbelt, breastplate, shoes, shield, helmet, sword, and lance. There were seven pieces in all.

As we learned in our last two lessons, there's a real devil out there, and he is violently against us. But when we are dressed in the whole armor of God, we are able to stand against him and all his cohorts. Instead of running from him, we are able to chase after him in the power of the Spirit. With the weapons of our warfare, we can push the enemy back and stand confidently in God's power.

The Real Meaning of the Word 'Wrestle'

When we come to Ephesians 6:12, the apostle Paul continues to speak by divine revelation, describing how the devil's power is arranged against us. He said, "For we wrestle not against flesh and blood, but against principalities, against powers, against the rulers of the darkness of this world, against spiritual wickedness in high places." There are several important words to understand in this verse, especially the word "wrestle."

When many people read the words, "For we wrestle not," they immediately think of two men in colorful outfits grappling in the middle of a square arena, each trying to pin the other to the mat for a three-second count. But that is not what it means. The word "wrestle" here in Greek is the word *pale*, and it is the only place in Scripture it is ever used. Thus, Paul was highly selective when he chose it. The word *pale* depicts a strong image of *struggling, wrestling,* or *hand-to-hand fighting*. Most importantly, it is the Greek word from which the Greeks derived the word *Palaestra*, which was a famous house of combat sports.

The *Palaestra* was a huge building that outwardly looked like a palace. But it was a palace of combat sports, dedicated to the cultivation of athletic skills. Every major Greek and Roman city had a gymnasium and a *Palaestra*. Regular competitors went to the gym, but only the most committed, determined, and daring athletes of that day could be found in the *Palaestra*. And they were there every morning, afternoon, and night, working out and training in this fabulous facility.

The Three Sports of the Palaestra

There were primarily three kinds of athletes that worked out and competed at the *Palaestra*: *boxers*, *wrestlers*, and *pankratiasts*. Let's take a look at each of these exceedingly dangerous and barbaric sports.

Boxing

The early boxers were not like the boxers today. They were extremely violent — so violent that they were not permitted to box without wearing helmets. Without the protection of helmets, their heads would have been crushed. Of all the sports, the ancients viewed boxing as the most hazardous and deadly.

These boxers were so brutal and barbaric that they wore gloves ribbed with steel and spiked with nails! At times, the steel wrapped around their gloves was serrated, like a hunting knife, in order to make deep gashes in the skin of an opponent. And as time went on, boxers began using gloves that were heavier and much more damaging.

In addition to this, it was not unusual for a boxer to hit his opponent's face so hard, with his thumb extended toward the eyes, that it knocked the opponent's eye right out of its socket! Believe it or not, even though this sport was so combative and violent, there were no rules — except that a boxer could not clench his opponent's fist. That was the only rule to the game! There were no "rounds" like there are in boxing today. The fight just went on and on, and continued until one of the two boxers surrendered or died in the ring.

If you study the artwork from the time of the early Greeks, it is quite common to see boxers whose faces, ears, and noses were totally deformed because of the dangerous gloves they wore. You will also frequently see paintings of boxers with blood pouring from their noses and with deep lacerations on their faces as a result of the serrated metal and spiked nails on the gloves. Few boxers in the ancient world ever lived to retire from their profession. Most of them died in the ring. An inscription from the First Century said of boxing: "A boxer's victory is obtained through blood." Indeed, this was a thoroughly violent sport

Wrestling

Like boxers, wrestlers had virtually no rules and often wrestled to the death. In fact, a favorite tactic in those days was to grab hold of an opponent around the waist, throw him up in the air, and quickly break his backbone in half from behind!

Wrestlers were tolerant of every imaginable tactic including breaking fingers, breaking ribs with a waist-lock, gouging the face, knocking out the eyes, and so forth. Even choking was an acceptable practice. Although less injurious than the other combat sports, wrestling was still a bitter struggle to the end. Wrestling was a very violent, bloody sport.

Pankration

Then there were *pankratiasts* who competed in the sport of *pankration*. This word is taken from two Greek words — the word *pan*, which means *all*, and the word *kratos*, which means *exhibited power*. When these words are compounded to form the word *pankration*, it described *someone with massive amounts of power*. These were men who claimed to have more power and might than everyone else.

This, indeed, was the purpose of *pankration*. Its competitors had already survived several rounds of boxing and wrestling and were out to prove they could not be beaten and were tougher than anyone else! In order to prove this, they kicked, punched, bit, gouged, broke fingers, broke legs, and did many other horrible things. Having basically no rules, *pankration* was a virtual free-for-all. They could do anything to any part of their competitor's body.

An early inscription from a father to his sons who participated in pankration said: "If you should hear that your son has died, believe it. But if you hear he has been defeated and retired, do not believe it." Why? Because more competitors died in this sport than surrendered or were defeated. Like the other combat sports, it was extremely violent.

Paul's Readers Vividly Understood What He Was Saying

So when the apostle Paul said, "For we wrestle not against flesh and blood," he used the word *pale* — translated here as "wrestle" — to illustrate and describe the intensity of our conflict with unseen, demonic powers that have been marshaled against us for our destruction.

By using this word "wrestle" — the old Greek word *pale* — Paul conveys the idea of a bitter struggle and a severe conflict. In other words, he is describing our warfare with demonic forces as a combat sport similar to those fought in the ancient *Palaestra*! Whoever fights the hardest and the meanest and whoever lasts the longest is the winner in your confrontation with the enemy. Therefore, you'd better be equipped, alert, and prepared before the fight begins.

New Testament believers understood exactly what Paul was communicating through the use of the word *pale* — wrestle. The combat sports of the *Palaestra* were famous in every city, and everyone knew about the notorious athletes who competed. First-Century believers understood the meaning of the word *pale* in the same way most Americans understand the meaning of the word "football." As soon as someone says "football," images of the field, the goal posts, the end zones, the stadium, and the game all flash on the screen of people's minds. Paul's readers had the same vivid understanding of what it meant to "wrestle."

For Christians, our real adversaries are an unseen host that is working behind the scenes. Who are these evil forces that are constantly working behind the scenes to seduce, deceive, control, and manipulate the flesh and the mind? The Bible says they are principalities, powers, rulers of the darkness of this world, and spiritual wickedness in high places.

Our Conflict Is Up-close and Personal

Before we examine the four categories of demonic powers, first take notice of the word "against," which is repeated five times in Ephesians 6:12. Paul said, "For we wrestle not against flesh and blood, but against principalities, against powers, against the rulers of the darkness of this world, against spiritual wickedness in high places."

The word "against" is not the Greek word *anti*, but rather the Greek word *pros*, and it describes *a close confrontation* or *a face-to-face encounter*. This is the very word used in John 1:1 to describe the preincarnate relationship between God the Father and Jesus. It says, "In the beginning was the Word, and the Word was with God, and the Word was God." The word "with" is the Greek word *pros* — the same word that is translated as "against" five times in Ephesians 6:12.

Now this same word of intimacy, this word that is used to denote a face-to-face relationship between the Father and the Son, is used to describe a face-to-face encounter with unseen, demonic spirits that have come to assault us. This means that spiritual warfare is not just what happens to people on the mission field or in the dark, inner-city regions. It is a supernatural battle that will happen at some point in the lives of all Christians. Each of us will come into direct, face-to-face contact with evil forces.

With this understanding, Ephesians 6:12 could thus be translated:

> **We wrestle not against flesh and blood, but face to face with principalities, eyeball to eyeball with powers, head-on with rulers of the darkness of this world, and shoulder to shoulder with spiritual wickedness in high places.**

Many scholars agree that the language of Ephesians 6:12 is militaristic language. It seems Paul had a revelation of how Satan's kingdom has been aligned militarily, and he captured the insights God gave him in his letter to the church of Ephesus.

WE WILL COME FACE TO FACE WITH…

'Principalities'

The first category of underworld forces Paul names is "principalities." In Greek, this is the word *archas*, which was used symbolically to denote *ancient times*, *the very beginning*, or *the origin*. It was also used to depict *individuals who hold the highest and loftiest position of rank and authority*. It is the word for *princes* or *principalities*.

But using the word *archas* — translated here as "principalities" — Paul is telling us at the very top of Satan's domain, there is a group of ruling demon spirits that are like *princes* or *principalities*, and they've held their lofty positions of power since ancient times.

'Powers'

The second category of demonic forces we see is "powers." This is a translation of the Greek word *exousia*, which describes *delegated authority* or *influence*. This word denotes *one who has received delegated power* and is often translated *authorities*. Furthermore, the word *exousia* could also denote *those who wielded authority entrusted to them by their superiors*.

So immediately underneath the high-ranking principalities that have been around since the very beginning, a second category of evil spiritual forces called "powers" have received a license — or authority — to carry out all manner of evil and wickedness. They're like roaming spirits about the earth, doing whatever they want to do.

'The Rulers of the Darkness of This World'

The next group of enemies from hell that we come up against is described as "the rulers of the darkness of this world." This phrase is a translation of the Greek word *kosmokrator*, which is a compound of the words *kosmos* and *kratos*. The word *kosmos* denotes something *ordered* and *arranged*, and the word *kratos* describes *raw power*. When these words are compounded to form *kosmokrator*, it describes *evil powers that have been organized and arranged against us*.

What's interesting is that this is the very word for *military training camps where young men were assembled, trained, and turned into a mighty army*. The new recruits were taught discipline and order, and all that manpower was converted into an organized, disciplined army. Thus, the word *kosmokrator* — translated here as "the rulers of the darkness of this world" — describes raw power that has been harnessed and developed into *a highly trained and aggressive force.*

The apostle Paul uses this word to tell us how serious the devil is about victimizing the human race. He takes demon spirits, which are like raw evil power, and harnesses them into organized forces. He then sends them forth against us to steal, kill, and destroy whatever and whoever they can. This shows us the devil's dedication to victimize and take down the human race.

'Spiritual Wickedness in High Places'

Paul rounds out his list of evil forces, describing them as "spiritual wickedness in high places." The word "wickedness" is a translation of the Greek word *poneria*, which describes *destruction, disaster, harm, or danger*. It can also depict something *malicious or malignant*; *foul, vile, hostile*, and *vicious*. It is not only that which is dangerous to the physical body, but also that which is dangerous to the spirit or mind. This word *poneria* was also used to depict *animals that are savage, wild, vicious, and dangerous.*

It is significant that Paul saves this Greek word until the end of this verse. By doing so, he is revealing to us the ultimate aim of Satan's dark domain: These demon spirits are sent forth from the spirit realm to afflict humanity in all manner of bad, vile, malevolent, vicious, and malignant ways. Having divine revelation of this archenemy is why Paul said...

> **"Put on the whole armour of God, that ye may be able to stand against the wiles of the devil."**
>
> **Ephesians 6:11**

In our next lesson, we will take a look at what Paul said in Ephesians 6:13 and see how God views you as a champion in Christ.

STUDY QUESTIONS

Study to shew thyself approved unto God, a workman that needeth not to be ashamed, rightly dividing the word of truth.
— 2 Timothy 2:15

1. Prior to this teaching, what was your understanding of the words, "For we wrestle not against flesh and blood"?
2. Knowing that the word "wrestle" is the Greek word *pale* and refers to the violent combat sports of the *Palaestra*, how has your perspective of spiritual warfare changed?
3. What is your greatest takeaway from this lesson on *Wrestling With Principalities of Power?*

PRACTICAL APPLICATION

But be ye doers of the word, and not hearers only, deceiving your own selves.
—James 1:22

1. After listening to and reading through the descriptions of the ancient sports of boxing, wrestling, and pankration, what similarities are you able to see between them and the spiritual battles you have faced against the enemy?
2. Since Satan runs his demons through a military-like camp to harness their raw power and train them before he sends them out, what do you think we as Christians who are enlisted in God's army need to carry out our assignments? (Consider Second Timothy 3:16,17; Ephesians 4:11-16; and Hebrews 10:25.)
3. The reason the devil seems to rack up so many victories against the Church is not because we lack power. The problem is we lack commitment, organization, and discipline. Be honest: Where do you know you can — and need to — come up higher in these three areas? What practical steps can you take to begin getting stronger in these areas?

LESSON 6

TOPIC

The Champion God Sees You To Be

SCRIPTURES

Ephesians 6:13-18 — Wherefore take unto you the whole armour of God, that ye may be able to withstand in the evil day, and having done all, to stand. Stand therefore, having your loins girt about with truth, and having on the breastplate of righteousness; and your feet shod with the preparation of the gospel of peace; above all, taking the shield of faith, wherewith ye shall be able to quench all the fiery darts of the wicked. And take the helmet of salvation, and the sword of the Spirit, which is the word of God: praying always with all prayer and supplication in the Spirit….

GREEK WORDS

1. "wherefore"— **Διὰ τοῦτο** (*dia touto*): wherefore; on account of all that I've said; in response to all of this; consequently
2. "take unto you"— **ἀναλάβετε** (*analabete*): the words **ἀνά** (*ana*) and **λαμβάνω** (*lambano*); the word **ἀνά** (*ana*) means again, to repeat again, or up; the word **λαμβάνω** (*lambano*); means to take; compounded, to take up again; pictures something laying down that must be picked up again
3. "whole armour"— **πανοπλία** (*panoplia*): pictures a soldier fully dressed in his armor from head to toe; the full attire and weaponry of a soldier; included the loinbelt, breastplate, shoes, shield, helmet, sword, and lance
4. "that"— **ἵνα** (*hina*): indicates express purpose
5. "may be able"— **δύναμαι** (*dunamai*): enabled; empowered; derived from **δύναμις** (*dunamis*), which is the idea of explosive, superhuman power that comes with enormous energy and produces phenomenal, extraordinary, and unparalleled results
6. "withstand"— **ἀντιστῆναι** (*antistenai*): to stand against; to push against; to aggressively position oneself against
7. "evil"— **πονηρός** (*poneros*): destruction, disaster, harm, or danger; malicious or malignant; foul, vile, hostile, and vicious; an act, attitude, or purpose that is wicked, unholy, and impure; depicts animals that are savage, wild, vicious, and dangerous
8. "having done all"— **κατεργάζομαι** (*katergadzomai*): having brought everything to an ultimate conclusion
9. "stand"— **στῆναι** (*stenai*): to stand; pictures a victorious soldier standing upright

SYNOPSIS

In addition to the magnificent collection of western European weaponry started by Emperor Alexander I, there is another outstanding assortment of armory in Russia. It is located in Moscow, deep inside the Kremlin, and it features weapons that are encrusted with rubies, emeralds, turquoise, pearls, and even diamonds. There are 24 karat gold sabers that are encrusted with jewels and shields that are covered with gems. These lavish weapons were worn by the czar as he rode on his steed through the streets of Moscow to show the people of Russia how powerful he was.

In the same way, when we're dressed in the whole armor of God, we shine with the power and might of Almighty God. We have no reason to be afraid or to be ashamed. We can throw our shoulders back and hold our heads high, knowing that God has provided us with all that we need to be victorious against the enemy. In His eyes, we are champions in the making!

The emphasis of this lesson:

Like the Ephesian believers, there are times in our lives when we walk away from the power of God and lay down our spiritual weaponry. In those moments, we must come to our senses and take up again the armor of God in order to be able to push back the forces of evil in the day we are savagely attacked.

We Are in a Real War Fighting Against a Real Enemy

In our first five lessons, we carefully examined the meaning of Ephesians 6:10 and 11, in which Paul said, "Finally, my brethren, be strong in the Lord and in the power of his might. Put on the whole armour of God, that ye may be able to stand against the wiles of the devil."

Then we looked at Paul's revelation about the military structure of Satan's forces that are arranged against us. He said, "For we wrestle not against flesh and blood, but against principalities, against powers, against the rulers of the darkness of this world, against spiritual wickedness in high places" (Ephesians 6:12).

In this verse, Paul used the Greek word *pale* — translated here as "wrestle" — to paint a clear picture of the intensity of our warfare against Satan.

The word *pale* is only used one time in the entire New Testament, and it is taken from the word *Palaestra*, which was the name given to a house of combat sports. Every major Greek and Roman city of the First Century had a *Palaestra*, and inside these fabulous facilities, three primary athletic contests took place: boxing, wrestling, and pankration. All these sports were back-snapping, eye-gouging, blood-spilling activities.

Again, Paul used this word to illustrate the seriousness of spiritual warfare. He was not trying to scare us, but to prepare us and wake us up to the fact that the enemy is real; and if we want to be victorious against him, we have to be *strong in the Lord* and allow His power to dress us in the supernatural armor God has provided.

Our Fight Is Face to Face

Although some Christians think that the battle only rages in foreign lands or in dark areas of inner cities, that is not the case. Again and again, we are told that we are fighting "...*against* principalities, *against* powers, *against* the rulers of the darkness of this world, *against* spiritual wickedness in high places" (Ephesians 6:12). This word "against" is the Greek word *pros*, and it describes *a close confrontation* or *a face-to-face encounter.*

Interestingly, this is the same word used in John 1:1 to describe the relationship between God the Father and Jesus His Son before He took on human form. It says, "In the Beginning was the Word, and the Word was with God, and the Word was God." The word "with" is the Greek word *pros* — the same word that is translated "against" five times in Ephesians 6:12.

Paul used this word *pros* — the word that denotes intimacy and closeness between the Father and the Son — to let us know that at some point in our Christian experience, we are going to be drawn into a very close conflict with evil. We will be face to face with principalities, eyeball to eyeball with powers, shoulder to shoulder with the rulers of the darkness of this world, and ribcage to ribcage with spiritual wickedness in high places.

Of course, you have no reason to be afraid because "...Greater is he that is in you, than he that is in the world" (1 John 4:4), and "...The weapons of [your] warfare are not carnal, but *mighty* through God to the pulling down of strong holds" (2 Corinthians 10:4). We simply need to realize what we are up against and cultivate the commitment, organization, and determination we need to abide in Christ and fight in His might.

In Response to All Paul Has Said...

In Ephesians 6:13, the apostle Paul went on to say, "Wherefore take unto you the whole armour of God, that ye may be able to withstand in the evil day, and having done all, to stand." The word "wherefore" in this verse is the Greek words *dia touto*, which means *wherefore* but can also be translated, *"On account of all I've said to you," "In response to all of this,"* or *consequently*.

What did Paul just say in the previous verses? First, he told the Ephesian believers that they needed to "...Be strong in the Lord, and in the power of His might" (*see* Ephesians 6:10). The same is true for us. Without the *dunamis* power of God energizing us, we are powerless against the enemy. We need God's power to carry our spiritual weaponry and to wield it effectively.

In Ephesians 6:11, Paul began to describe "the whole armor of God," which He has given us. The seven pieces of our armor include the belt of truth, breastplate of righteousness, shoes of peace, shield of faith, helmet of salvation, sword of the Spirit, and lance of prayer. Paul said when we put on the whole armor of God, we're "able to stand against the wiles of the devil."

Then in verse 12, Paul gave us a vivid picture of the devil's powers that are marshaled against us. Indeed, Satan and his forces are committed, organized, and disciplined, and he has dispatched evil into the lower regions of the atmosphere to distress and victimize the entire human race. After saying all this, Paul inserted the word "wherefore." It is the equivalent of him saying, "In light of all of this..."; "In light of everything I've just said to you..."; or "Consequently, in response to all of this...." Then Paul said, "...Take unto you the whole armour of God..." (Ephesians 6:13).

One of the Saddest Statements in the New Testament

If there was ever a statement that sadly depicts the condition of many Christians, it is the phrase "take unto you," which appears in Ephesians 6:13. This phrase is a translation of the Greek word *analabete*, which is a command that comes from the words *ana* and *lambano*. The word *ana* means *again*, *to repeat again*, or *up*; and the word *lambano* means *to take*. When these words are compounded to form the word *analabete*, it means *to take up again*. It pictures *something laying down that must be picked up again.*

In this verse, the apostle Paul is speaking directly to his readers in Ephesus — and to believers of all generations, which includes us. And he is saying, "Hey, take up again (*analabete*) the whole armor of God. You've laid down your spiritual weapons because you've dropped your power. Pick it up again." We know they were not walking in the power of God, because if they were "strong in the Lord," they would have been dressed in their spiritual armor. Remember, it is the power of God that equips us.

As long as you're walking in God's power, you're going to be clothed in spiritual armor. That's why Paul said, "Put on the whole armour of God..." (Ephesians 6:11). The phrase "put on" is the Greek word *enduo*, and it describes *the power of a whole army being deposited into you*. It is *inner strengthening*, or *supernatural enablement* to do supernatural, superhuman things. When this divine power comes into you, the power of God begins to dress you in spiritual weaponry.

The Ephesian believers had laid down the divine power of God, and Paul was telling them, "Take it up again — *analabete*! Take it up now!" These were believers who once walked in the victorious power of God and were dressed in divine weaponry. But they had laid it down and walked away from the red hot, blazing passion they once had for Jesus. They had become monotonous Christians, just going through the motions, and their lives were a mess.

The Ephesian Believers Had Lost Their First Love

As we've noted in previous lessons, when Paul wrote his letter to the Ephesian believers, they were grieving the Holy Spirit by what they were doing. Many had gotten caught up in gossip and malicious backbiting. Because of pride, they were harboring unforgiveness and bitterness toward one another. Some of these church members had become lazy and would not work. Others had even stooped to stealing. The apostle Paul pointed out all these things in Ephesians 4. Indeed, this was not the picture of victorious believers. What happened to them?

According to Acts 19, the church of Ephesus had been born in the supernatural power of God. Through a great spiritual awakening, people were healed, people were saved, and demons were cast out. These believers were walking in divine power and dressed in divine weaponry. But somewhere along the way, they began to drift away from their devotion to the Lord.

Jesus actually confirmed this in Revelation 2:4 when He Himself addressed the church of Ephesus saying, "Nevertheless I have somewhat against thee, because thou hast left thy first love." By leaving their first love, the Ephesian believers had let go of the *dunamis* power of God and were no longer dressed in their spiritual armor. In His great love, Jesus told them, "Remember therefore from whence thou art fallen, and repent, and do the first works..." (Revelation 2:5).

In the same way, Paul commanded these same Christians to "take up again (*analabete*) the whole armor of God" and *repeat* or *do again* what they were doing when they were passionately serving Christ. These instructions are for you too. If you've laid down the power of God and your divine weaponry, He is urging you to "take it up again" — *analabete*! Go back to what you were doing in the beginning of your relationship with Jesus and repeat those actions.

The Whole Armor of God Enables You To 'Withstand in the Evil Day'

What did Paul command the Ephesian believers to pick up again? Ephesians 6:13 says "the whole armor of God." The phrase "whole armor" in Greek is the word *panoplia*, which is the compound of the words *pan* and *haplo*. The word *pan* means *all*, and the word *haplo* describes *weapons*. When these two words are compounded, it pictures *the full attire and weaponry of a soldier*; *a soldier fully dressed in his armor from head to toe*. This included the loinbelt, breastplate, shoes, shield, helmet, sword, and lance.

Even the word "that" is important. In Greek, it is the word *hina*, and it indicates *express purpose*. Paul is about ready to tell the Ephesian believers the *express purpose* for taking up again the whole armor of God, and it is so that "...ye may be able to withstand in the evil day..." (Ephesians 6:13).

The phrase "may be able" is the Greek word *dunamai*, which is a form of the word *dunamis*, and it means *enabled* or *empowered*. Being derived from the word *dunamis*, it carries the idea of *explosive, superhuman power that comes with enormous energy and produces phenomenal, extraordinary, and unparalleled results*.

The use of this word tells us that when you receive God's weapons of warfare, suddenly you become a walloping, conquering force. You're no longer running from the devil; now you're pursuing him and putting him on the run. You become filled with the full force of Heaven's army, and its might is released through you. Like a divine force of nature, you turn into God's hurricane, tornado, or earthquake that shakes up the domain of darkness.

With God's power, the Bibles says you are enabled to "…withstand in the evil day…" (Ephesians 6:13). The word "withstand" in Greek is *antistenai*, which means *to stand against*; *to push against*; or *to aggressively position oneself against*. It is a picture of a soldier who is moving forward to drive back the forces of darkness in the "evil day."

Now, there are a lot of "evil days" on the prophetic calendar. To understand what Paul was saying here, we need to know the meaning of the word "evil." In this verse, "evil" is the word *poneros*, and it depicts *destruction, disaster, harm,* or *danger*. It describes *something malicious or malignant* or *something that is foul, vile, hostile, and vicious*. It denotes *an act, attitude, or purpose that is wicked, unholy, and impure*. What is interesting is that this word *poneros* — translated here as "evil" — was the same word used to depict animals that are savage, wild, vicious, and dangerous.

Basically, Paul was saying, "Eventually a day is going to come when a lot of evil is going to try and get in your way. *Destruction, disaster, harm,* or *danger* is going to come and attempt to tear you apart like wild animals that are vicious and dangerous. What the enemy brings against you will be foul, vile, hostile, and malicious. But if you are dressed in God's divine weaponry, you can stand against it!"

Friend, we are children of God. Sickness does not belong to us. Neither does destruction, disaster, or any vile, malicious attack. If any of these things try to penetrate your day, you don't have to just grin and bear it. Instead, you can stand in the *kratos* power of God and say to the enemy, "You don't belong in my life or in my day, and I'm going to push you back (*antistenai*) across the line."

This is what Paul was saying. You don't have to be a victim any more. When you have the power of God and you're dressed in the whole armor of God you can stand against any evil that tries to get in your way. If evil tries to penetrate your finances, your health, your marriage, your relationships, your job, or your thinking — push it back! You don't have to take it anymore because God has given you everything you need to stand against evil that tries to penetrate your life.

'Having Done All, Stand'

The apostle Paul concludes Ephesians 6:13 saying, "…And having done all, to stand." Many Christians misinterpret what is being said here. They mistakenly believe Paul is saying, "If the power of God doesn't work, stand. If the weapons of our warfare don't work, stand. If you just keep standing, eventually you will outlast the enemy." But that is not what Paul is saying. The truth is, the power of God does work, and so do the weapons of our warfare.

When Paul said, "having done all," he used the Greek word *katergadzomai*, which literally means *having brought everything to an ultimate conclusion*. And the word "stand" is the Greek word *stenai*, which means *to stand*, and it pictures a victorious soldier standing upright.

In this verse, God is prophetically declaring what you are going to look like when your challenge is completed. From the beginning of the fight, He sees you as the champion that you really are. You're not a victim or a failure, and you're not going to be defeated by Satan. You are more than a conqueror in Jesus Christ!

Essentially, what Paul is saying in this verse is, "And having brought the whole battle to a conclusion, let me prophesy and tell you what I see from the very beginning. When this thing is all said and done, when it's all wrapped up, you're going to be the one standing." This is what will happen when you embrace God's power and allow Him to dress you in divine weaponry.

To all this, Paul lists each of the seven pieces of God's armor saying:

> **Stand therefore, having your loins girt about with truth, and having on the breastplate of righteousness; and your feet shod with the preparation of the gospel of peace; above all, taking the shield of faith, wherewith ye shall be able to quench all the fiery darts of the wicked. And take the helmet of salvation, and the sword of the Spirit, which is the word of God: praying always with all prayer and supplication in the Spirit….**
>
> **Ephesians 6:14-18**

In our next lesson, we will closely examine the first two pieces of spiritual weaponry — the loinbelt of truth and the breastplate of righteousness.

STUDY QUESTIONS

Study to shew thyself approved unto God, a workman that needeth not to be ashamed, rightly dividing the word of truth.
— 2 Timothy 2:15

In every fight you face, God sees you from the very beginning as the champion you really are. There are many verses in the Bible where He prophetically declares what you are going to look like when your challenge is completed. Take time to reflect on these scriptures and allow the Holy Spirit to paint a fresh picture on the canvas of your heart of who you really are in Him.

- 2 Corinthians 2:14
- Psalm 44:4-8
- Romans 8:35-37
- 1 John 5:4

PRACTICAL APPLICATION

But be ye doers of the word, and not hearers only, deceiving your own selves.
— James 1:22

The believers in Ephesus were no longer walking in the power of God. They had laid down their spiritual weapons, and Paul urged them to take them up again. These were believers who once walked in the victorious power of God and were dressed in divine weaponry. But for some reason they had walked away from the red hot, blazing passion they once had for Jesus.

1. How about you? How would you describe the current condition of your relationship with Jesus?
2. Is your love and excitement for God and the things of God as fiery and full as the day you got saved? Or has your passion grown cold?
3. What have you experienced that has caused your fire to fizzle and left you drifting away from your devotion and dedication to Jesus?

4. If you've walked away from God's power and your love for Him has dwindled, Jesus says to you, "*Remember* therefore from whence thou art fallen, and *repent*, and do the first works..." (Revelation 2:5). What are some of the "first works" you once did when you first began your life with Jesus that you need to do again?

LESSON 7

TOPIC

The Loinbelt of Truth, Breastplate of Righteousness

SCRIPTURES

1. **Ephesians 6:14-18** — Stand therefore, having your loins girt about with truth, and having on the breastplate of righteousness; and your feet shod with the preparation of the gospel of peace; above all, taking the shield of faith, wherewith ye shall be able to quench all the fiery darts of the wicked. And take the helmet of salvation, and the sword of the Spirit, which is the word of God: praying always with all prayer and supplication in the Spirit....
2. **1 Peter 1:23** — Being born again, not of corruptible seed, but of incorruptible, by the word of God, which liveth and abideth for ever.
3. **2 Corinthians 5:21** — For he hath made him [Jesus] to be sin for us, who knew no sin; that we might be made the righteousness of God in him.

GREEK WORDS

1. "stand" — **στῆτε** (*stete*): to stand upright; pictures one so confident that he stands with his head held high and his shoulders thrown back
2. "loins" — **ὀσφύς** (*osphus*): the reproductive area; the seat of regenerative powers
3. "girt about" — **περιζώννυμι** (*peridzonnumi*): to fasten a girdle around; to girt oneself for action
4. "breastplate" — **θώραξ** (*thurax*): a breastplate that covered the part of the body from the neck to the navel; it protected the chest and

extended down to the hips and consisted of two parts and protected the body on both sides from the neck to the middle; it protected vital organs; figuratively, it protects the heart

SYNOPSIS

As we saw in the opening of our last lesson, there is another armor collection deep inside the Kremlin in Moscow, and it is simply spectacular. Tightly secured in glass cabinets, there are sabers, shields, daggers, spears, and even breastplates that are encrusted with precious stones like emeralds, rubies, gold, turquoise, and diamonds. These dazzling weapons were worn by the Russian czar as he paraded through the streets of Moscow and attended special ceremonies. This armor was intended to display his power, his majesty, and his wealth.

As remarkable as the weaponry in the Moscow Armory Museum is, it cannot compare to the magnificence of the spiritual armor we have been provided through Jesus Christ! As a royal ambassador of Heaven, you've been given weapons of even greater value than these, and they are described in Ephesians 6:14-18. There are seven weapons in all, and the first two weapons — the loinbelt of truth and the breastplate of righteousness — are described in verse 14.

The emphasis of this lesson:

The loinbelt of truth is our most important piece of weaponry. It is the only tangible piece of armor, and it holds all the other pieces firmly in place. The breastplate of righteousness protects our vital organs, keeping us emotionally stable and strong. The longer we wear it, the more brilliantly we reflect the Son and more blinding we become to the enemy.

A Review of Ephesians 6:10-13

Before Paul unveiled all the particulars of our divine weaponry, he first talked about our need for spiritual power (*see* Ephesians 6:10). A weak person cannot carry the armor of God, much less put it to effective use. Hence, we must first be strong in the Lord in order to operate in the armor of God.

In our empowered position, Paul commanded us to "Put on the whole armour of God, that ye may be able to stand against the wiles of the devil"

(Ephesians 6:11). In this verse, we saw how the enemy operates on a single lane of attack, building a road that is headed straight for our mind. His ultimate aim is to penetrate and then scramble our thinking, taking us captive through his deceptions. This is why we need to be dressed in God's whole armor.

Then in Ephesians 6:12, Paul explained how Satan's kingdom is militarily aligned into four specific categories: principalities, powers, the rulers of the darkness, and spiritual wickedness in high places. This verse lets us know that spiritual warfare is not just what happens to people on the mission field or in dark, inner-cities. It is a supernatural, face-to face fight that will happen at some point in the lives of all Christians.

In Ephesians 6:13, we learned that sometimes believers drop or lay down their weapons. If we have done that, we need to ask God for a fresh infilling of His divine power and pick up our weapons again. It is only through the power of God and His divine weaponry that we can effectively withstand the enemy in the evil day.

The apostle Paul went on to say, "…And having done all, to stand" (Ephesians 6:13). Many Christians mistakenly believe Paul is saying, "If the power of God and the weapons of our warfare don't work, stand." But that is not what Paul is saying. The phrase "having done all" in Greek literally means *having brought everything to an ultimate conclusion*. And the word "stand" is the Greek word *stenai*, which means *to stand*, and it pictures a victorious soldier standing upright.

In this verse, God is prophetically declaring what you're going to look like when your challenge is completed. From the beginning of the fight, God sees you as the champion you really are. You're not a victim or a failure. You are more than a conqueror in Jesus Christ! And when this challenge is finished, you're going to be the one standing. This is what will happen when you embrace God's power and allow Him to dress you in divine weaponry.

Stand Therefore and Be Dressed in God's Armor

In Ephesians 6:14, the apostle Paul begins listing and describing the seven pieces of spiritual weaponry. But before he does, he first tells us, "Stand therefore…." The word "stand" here is the Greek word *stete*, which means *to stand upright.* It pictures *a Roman soldier who confidently stands with his head held high and his shoulders thrown back.*

This lets us know that when we are equipped in the full armor of God, we have every reason to stand up straight and be confident in God! We don't have to be slumped over or worried that we're not going to make it. We can stand tall, hold our head high, throw our shoulders back, and be assured and confident — not in ourselves, but in the power and the weapons God has provided us.

Paul names all seven pieces of our spiritual armor in Ephesians 6:14-18: "Stand therefore, having your loins girt about with truth, and having on the breastplate of righteousness; and your feet shod with the preparation of the gospel of peace; above all, taking the shield of faith, wherewith ye shall be able to quench all the fiery darts of the wicked. And take the helmet of salvation, and the sword of the Spirit, which is the word of God: praying always with all prayer and supplication in the Spirit....

According to this passage, every Christian is equipped with the loinbelt of truth, breastplate of righteousness, shoes of peace, shield of faith, helmet of salvation, sword of the Spirit, and lance of prayer. These pieces of armor parallel the armor of a Roman soldier and are powerful at protecting and defending us against enemy attacks.

The Loinbelt of Truth: Our Most Important Piece of Armor

The first and most important piece of weaponry God has provided us is the *loinbelt of truth.* Paul said, "Stand therefore, having your loins girt about with truth..." (Ephesians 6:14). Notice this archaic sounding word "loins." It is the Greek word *osphus,* which describes *the reproductive area* or *the seat of regenerative powers.* And the words "girt about" are a translation of the Greek word *peridzonnumi,* which means *to fasten a girdle around* or *to girt oneself for action.*

Of all seven pieces of armor the Roman soldier wore, the loinbelt was the least attractive, the least noticeable, and the most boring piece! When a Roman soldier was wearing his beautiful breastplate of brass and his brightly flumed helmet, who would notice his belt?

Think about it. If you were to describe a man's clothing, would you begin with his belt? You can hardly even see it. You would probably start out by describing his jacket; then you'd move on to his shirt, his necktie, and even his shoes. But you wouldn't begin with his belt, would you?

Although a person's belt may seem to be insignificant, it isn't. In many cases, taking off your belt will result in your pants starting to fall down, your shirt coming untucked, and even getting tripped up and falling face first to the floor. Without a belt, you'd probably spend a lot of your time trying to hold yourself together. You would not feel very confident, and you certainly wouldn't want to make any fast moves!

That is precisely what the loinbelt did for the Roman soldier — it held all the pieces of his armor together. For example, the Roman soldier's breastplate was made of a piece of metal (usually brass) that went down the front and another piece that went down the back. But without the loinbelt to secure it in place, it would flap around when he rushed forward in battle.

Likewise, the soldier's massive shield rested on a clip on one side of the loinbelt when it was not in use, and his sword was attached to another clip on the other side. On the back of his loinbelt, a pouch was attached that housed his lances. Clearly, without the loinbelt fixed in its place around his waist, the soldier's armor would have literally fallen apart, piece by piece.

In the same way, the loinbelt of truth — which is *the written Word of God* — is the most important piece of spiritual weaponry we have. It is central to everything and holds all the other pieces of our armor firmly in place. Without God's Word wrapped around us, we wouldn't have God's peace (our shoes). Without God's Word in our lives, we would cease to feel the joy of our salvation (our helmet), and our sense of righteousness (our breastplate) would eventually evaporate. Equally, if we lay aside the belt of truth, we would quickly lose our ability to walk in faith (our shield), and our sword of the Spirit would be lost. When we ignore the Word of God and cease to apply it to our life on a daily basis, we have willfully chosen to let our entire spiritual life come apart at the seams!

The Bible Is the Only Visible, Tangible Piece of Spiritual Armor

The loinbelt of truth is the written Word of God! Although the majority of our spiritual armor is *invisible,* **the Bible is the only piece of weaponry that is tangible to hold and visible to the eye.** It is the only spiritual weapon that God has permitted to take on a physical, natural form and pass tangibly from the spirit realm into our hands! *That is how important it is for us to have the Word of God in our possession. It is the most vital piece of weaponry that we possess.*

For instance, you can't physically see the breastplate of righteousness. Likewise, you can't physically see your shoes of peace, your shield of faith, your helmet of salvation, your sword of the Spirit, or your lance of intercession. These are *invisible weapons.* But you can see one weapon... the loinbelt of truth — the Bible. The Holy Spirit inspired Paul to go straight to the middle of the soldier and begin describing the armor of God by first mentioning the soldier's belt. And by that, God is saying that the piece of armor that is in the middle of the man — the loinbelt of truth — is *the most important weapon.*

Friend, you absolutely cannot function victoriously as a believer without the Word of God having an active and central role in your life. You may run on steam from the past for a while, but you won't run very far. If you remove the loinbelt — the Word of God — it will only be a matter of time until you begin to fall to pieces spiritually. Demonic assaults will break through that invisible barrier that used to protect you, and chaos will take over in your life.

Do you want to succeed spiritually? Do you want to be spiritually equipped? Then you must begin by taking up the Word of God and permanently affixing it to your life. You have to give it a central place and a dominant role, allowing it to be the "loinbelt" that holds the rest of your weaponry together. The Bible must be the governor, the law, the ruler, and "the final say-so" in your life.

The Word of God Provides Us With Reproductive Power

Looking once more at Ephesians 6:14, it says, "Stand therefore, having your loins girt about with truth..." (Ephesians 6:14). As mentioned earlier, the word "loins" is the Greek word *osphus*, which describes *the reproductive area* or *the seat of regenerative powers.* The loinbelt covered the soldier's loins — effectively protecting his reproductive organs. This was worn to preserve his ability to reproduce. One damaging kick in this area from an enemy meant that soldier would never have children.

Because the loinbelt is representative of the Word of God and the loinbelt was historically a protection to the reproductive abilities of a man, this tells us something else very significant. It plainly shows us that our ability to produce for God is directly tied to our relationship with the Word of God.

You become sterile spiritually if you don't have God's Word actively operating in your life. You do nothing; you produce nothing; you demonstrate no anointing or healing power. When you get out of the Word of God, you are reduced to a state of spiritual barrenness. Can you see why the Holy Spirit started with the belt when He described our weaponry in Ephesians 6?

The Word of God contains the reproductive ability of God. First Peter 1:23 confirms this saying, "Being born again, not of corruptible seed, but of incorruptible, by the word of God, which liveth and abideth for ever." When you are in the Word, the Word gets in you and you become impregnated with the very life of God. It is the Word operating in your life that gives you the ability to supernaturally produce all that God is — in you and in others.

The Breastplate of Righteousness Provides Heart Protection and Emotional Stability

In addition to wrapping the loinbelt of truth tightly around our waist, we are also instructed to put on the "breastplate of righteousness" (*see* Ephesians 6:14). In Greek, the word for "breastplate" is *thorax*, and it depicted *a breastplate that covered the part of the body from the neck to the navel.* It protected the chest and extended down to the hips. It consisted of two parts and protected the body on both sides — front and back— from the neck to the mid-section. Most importantly, it protected vital organs; figuratively, it protects the heart.

The breastplate was the most beautiful piece of weaponry that the Roman soldier possessed and at the same time, it was the heaviest piece that he wore. As conspicuous as the soldier's helmet was, the piece of armor that immediately caught the attention of onlookers was not his helmet, but his large, shiny, gorgeous breastplate.

Something quite remarkable took place when a soldier walked while wearing his breastplate. It was fashioned with row upon row of bronze or brass strips that were like the scales of a fish, and when the soldier marched around, all those pieces of metal would rub against each other, creating a brilliant luster to the breastplate. The longer a soldier walked around with his breastplate on, the shinier and more brilliant his breastplate became.

As a believer, Jesus has made you righteous. The Bible says, "For he [God] hath made him [Jesus] to be sin for us, who knew no sin; that we might be made the righteousness of God in him (2 Corinthians 5:21). Righteousness is not something we have obtained on our own. God gives it to us by grace. Paul said, "But if Christ lives in you, [then although] your [natural] body is dead by reason of sin and guilt, the spirit is alive **because of [the] righteousness [that He imputes to you]**" (Romans 8:10 *AMPC*).

When a person doesn't know he or she is righteous, that person usually lacks confidence and prays very defeated prayers. On the other hand, when a person really knows he or she is the righteousness of God in Christ, that person shines and dazzles with confidence. Not because they are confident in themselves, but because they are confident in the righteousness God has given them.

Furthermore, knowing we are righteous in Christ powerfully protects our heart, which is the seat of our emotions. The truth is our emotions can be all over the place — up one minute and down the next. But when we are covered by the breastplate of righteousness, we remain emotionally stable and strong. And the longer we walk in righteousness, the more brilliant we become.

Being Mindful of Your Righteousness in Christ Is Blinding to the Enemy

Something else is quite amazing about the breastplate. Being made of brass, its golden color shined and sparkled when it was out in the sun. Therefore, when the fully-armed soldier went outside on a sunny day, the rays of the sun would reflect off his breastplate and create a dazzling spectacle.

It's like driving in your car on a bright and sunny day, when suddenly the sun gleams off an outside piece of metal and begins glaring into your eyes. It is so powerful you can hardly see the road. If you've experienced this, you can imagine what it would have been like to walk past a Roman soldier clothed in his brass breastplate with all that added shine and luster!

When a Roman soldier walked out into the afternoon sunlight, he must have looked like a rainbow, casting beams wherever he went! What do you suppose it was like when an entire legion of Roman soldiers walked out into the sunshine? The whole mountainside or valley where they were marching would begin to shine as they moved forward in their bright and gleaming breastplates! It would have been so glorious that the enemy would have been blinded and unable to see to fight. Thus, the breastplate became a powerful weapon of offense.

Had the breastplate been stored in a dark room and never used, it still would have been beautiful simply because it was made out of brass. But because the soldier used his breastplate and walked around wearing it, it became even more beautiful with time. The same is true for you as a believer.

The more you wear your breastplate of righteousness, walking through life fully conscious of your righteousness in Christ, the more brightly you will shine as a light in a dark world of sin. As you walk in righteousness, all you have to do is walk into a dark situation, and that darkness will begin to flee from you. Evil forces always flee from righteousness because they cannot endure the brilliant light that righteousness reflects into their eyes!

The devil wants to assault us. He wants to tell us that we're not righteous and that we're of no value to God or to man. This is why the Holy Spirit tells us that we have righteousness as a "breastplate" to protect us. When you know that God has made you righteous — when you have your breastplate of righteousness fixed firmly in place — it doesn't matter how many arrows the enemy shoots against you because not one of them will penetrate. No word of condemnation, no false allegation, and no guilty thought will penetrate your heart or lodge in your mind when you are walking in your breastplate of righteousness.

When you understand that God has freely imparted righteousness to you and that this God-given righteousness now serves you as a gorgeous breastplate, it will affect your attitude profoundly. You will discover that your level of confidence rises dramatically because an attitude of righteousness imparts both confidence and tremendous authority. With that confidence in operation, you will move out to do all kinds of exploits for God. Righteousness will equip you not only in a spiritual way, but it will affect you in the natural realm as well. Righteousness will make you noticeable. You are as brilliant and powerful as Jesus Himself when you are wearing this breastplate!

In our next lesson, we will turn our attention to the next two pieces of spiritual weaponry: the *shoes of peace* and the *shield of faith.*

STUDY QUESTIONS

Study to shew thyself approved unto God, a workman that needeth not to be ashamed, rightly dividing the word of truth.
— 2 Timothy 2:15

1. What fascinating new facts did you learn about the *loinbelt of truth*? How about the *breastplate of righteousness*? How do these fresh insights help you better understand the purpose and practical uses of these pieces of weaponry?
2. No book on planet earth is more powerful and life-giving than the Bible! Jesus is the Word wrapped in flesh, and the Bible is the Word wrapped in print. When you take in Scripture, you literally take in Jesus! Look at these verses and see what a daily diet of God's Word provides:
   - Deuteronomy 8:3; Psalm 119:103; Proverbs 4:20-22; Jeremiah 15:16; 1 Peter 2:2
   - 2 Timothy 3:16,17; Psalm 19:7-11 and 119:105
   - Psalm 119:9; John 15:3 and 17:17; Ephesians 5:26
   - Romans 1:16; Hebrews 4:12; James 1:21
   - Romans 15:4
3. According to Philippians 3:8 and 9, what are the two kinds of righteousness? Which one are you operating in — what do you believe makes you righteous? (Also consider Romans 4:3-13 and Galatians 2:21.)
4. How do you think having a solid understanding of your righteousness in Christ affects the way you pray and the results of your prayers? (Consider First John 3:20-22 and 5:14,15.)

PRACTICAL APPLICATION

But be ye doers of the word, and not hearers only, deceiving your own selves.
—James 1:22

1. The soldier's loinbelt was the most important piece of weaponry. It attached to all the other pieces of armor and held them securely in place. The same is true of the *loinbelt of truth*, which is *the Word of God*. Be honest: How important is the Bible in your life? One of the greatest ways to accurately determine the priority you place on God's Word is by looking at your levels of peace, faith, joy, and your sense of righteousness. What do these indicators tell you? What changes can you make in your daily routine to invest more time reading and soaking in the Scripture?
2. When you look at yourself, what do you see? Do your past failures and weaknesses glare at you? Or do you see yourself the way God sees you — as the *righteousness of God in Christ Jesus*?
3. If you or someone you know is struggling with feelings of condemnation and guilt, meditate on these truths from Scripture and receive *by faith* the righteousness God graciously offers.
   - Romans 8:1,2
   - John 3:17,18
   - Romans 8:31-34

LESSON 8

TOPIC

The Shoes of Peace and Shield of Faith

SCRIPTURES

1. **Ephesians 6:14-18** — Stand therefore, having your loins girt about with truth, and having on the breastplate of righteousness; and your feet shod with the preparation of the gospel of peace; above all, taking

the shield of faith, wherewith ye shall be able to quench all the fiery darts of the wicked. And take the helmet of salvation, and the sword of the Spirit, which is the word of God: praying always with all prayer and supplication in the Spirit....

2. **Romans 16:20** — And the God of peace shall bruise Satan under your feet shortly....
3. **Romans 12:3** — ...God hath dealt to every man the measure of faith.
4. **Psalm 92:10** — ...I shall be anointed with fresh oil.

GREEK WORDS

1. "shod" — **ὑποδέω** (*hupodeo*): compound of the words **ὑπο** (*hupo*) and **δέω** (*deo*); the word **ὑπο** (*hupo*) means under, and **δέω** (*deo*) means to bind; compounded, bind something tightly on the bottom of one's feet
2. "preparation" — **ἑτοιμασία** (*etoimasia*): carries the idea of readiness for movement
3. "peace" — **εἰρήνη** (*eirene*): the cessation of war; conflict put away; a time of rebuilding and reconstruction after war has ceased; distractions removed; a time of prosperity; the rule of order in the place of chaos; it is a calm, inner stability that results in the ability to conduct oneself peacefully even in the midst of circumstances that would normally be traumatic or upsetting; it is the Greek equivalent for the Hebrew word shalom, which expresses the idea of wholeness, completeness or tranquility in the soul that is unaffected by outward circumstances or pressures
4. "bruise" — **συντρίβω** (*suntribo*): denotes the act of smashing and utterly crushing grapes into wine; the act of snapping, breaking, and crushing bones; pictures breaking bones so terribly that they can never be mended or healed, so that the bones have been utterly smashed and crushed beyond recognition
5. "shield" — **θυρεός** (*thureos*): a door that was wide in width and long in length; used to depict battle shields because these shields were shaped like a door, wide in width and long in length, just like the door of a house
6. "taking" — **ἀναλαμβάνω** (*analambano*): to pick something back up again; to lift back up into its correct position

7. "wicked" — **πονηρός** (*poneros*): malicious or malignant; foul, vile, hostile, and vicious; used to depict animals that are savage, wild, vicious, and dangerous

SYNOPSIS

Weapons have been around in one form or another for thousands of years. Nations have stockpiled them and even put them on display. Thus far, we have seen that Russia has two extraordinary collections of armor — one in the renowned Winter Palace in Saint Petersburg and a second one deep inside the Kremlin in Moscow. The collection in Moscow is called the Armory Museum, and it is filled with remarkable daggers, sabers, shields, breastplates, and arrows that are covered with precious gemstones including emeralds, rubies, turquoise, pearls, and diamonds. These weapons were worn by the Russian czar and members of nobility as a show of great power and wealth.

As amazing as these weapons are, they are nothing in comparison to the spiritual armor God has made available to you and all believers. These weapons are presented in Ephesians 6:14-18 and include seven pieces: the loinbelt of truth, breastplate of righteousness, shoes of peace, shield of faith, helmet of salvation, sword of the Spirit, and lance of prayer.

The emphasis of this lesson:

It is God's will for us to stand and walk in His peace, which is why He's given us shoes of peace as part of our armor. The shoes are both an offensive weapon of protection and a defensive weapon meant to pulverize the enemy. We have also been provided a customized shield of faith to protect us from the enemy's fiery arrows.

We Need God's Power and His Whole Armor

The apostle Paul began his teaching on spiritual warfare in Ephesians 6:10 by saying, "Finally, my brethren, be strong in the Lord, and in the power of his might." We learned that in order to be dressed in God's armor, we need to first be filled with God's power. Purposefully, Paul went on to say, "Put on the whole armour of God, that ye may be able to stand against the wiles of the devil" (Ephesians 6:11). The words "whole armour" are a translation of the Greek word *panoplia*, which is *the picture of a soldier fully dressed in his armor from head to toe.*

Why do we need the *whole armor* of God? So that we can stand against the wiles — or *mind games* — of the devil. The Bible says, "For we wrestle not against flesh and blood, but against principalities, against powers, against the rulers of the darkness of this world, against spiritual wickedness in high places" (Ephesians 6:12).

Paul goes on to say, "Wherefore take unto you the whole armour of God, that ye may be able to withstand in the evil day, and having done all, to stand" (Ephesians 6:13). For a second time, we hear God speak through Paul His strong desire for us to be outfitted in the "whole armor" — every piece of divine weaponry that He has made available. The word "wherefore" in this verse is the Greek words *dia touto*, which basically could be translated, "*On account of all that I've said to you,* take unto you the whole armor of God."

He Enables Us To Withstand in the Evil Day

In the latter part of verse 13, Paul tells us the reason for being dressed in the whole armor: "…That ye may be able to withstand in the evil day…." This begs the question, "What is an evil day?" It is any day you wake up and are met with something evil. If you wake up and you or your child is sick, evil has intruded into your day. If you suddenly find yourself facing an unexpected financial problem, evil has entered your day. With the power of God and His divine weaponry, you can "withstand" in the evil day, which means you are empowered *to push evil back across the line* and away from you. You can literally open your mouth and say, "Devil, this is my territory, not yours. In the name of Jesus and according to His Word, I push you back across the line and out of my life."

Paul then adds, "…And having done all, to stand" (Ephesians 6:13). Many Christians mistakenly believe Paul is saying, "If the power of God and the weapons of our warfare don't work, stand." But that is not what he is saying. The phrase "having done all" in the Greek literally means *having brought everything to an ultimate conclusion*. And the word "stand" is the Greek word *stenai*, which means *to stand*, and it pictures *a victorious soldier standing upright*.

In this verse, God prophetically declares what you're going to look like when your trial is finished. From the beginning of the fight, God sees you as the champion you really are. You're not defeated nor are you a failure. You're more than a conqueror in Jesus Christ! And when this challenge is done, you're going to be the one standing. This is what you can expect to happen when you embrace God's power and allow Him to dress you in divine weaponry.

We Have Every Reason To Be Confident

The way Paul ends verse 13 is the way he begins verse 14. He tells us, "Stand therefore..." (Ephesians 6:14). The word "stand" here is the Greek word *stete*, which means *to stand upright*. It pictures *a Roman soldier who confidently stands with his head held high and his shoulders thrown back*. Basically, Paul is saying, "Since you're going to be standing victoriously at the end of the fight, why not just begin standing victoriously now."

When we are dressed in the whole armor of God, we have every reason to stand up straight and be confident in God! We don't have to be depressed or worried that we're not going to make it. We can stand strong, hold our head high, throw our shoulders back, and be assured and confident — not in ourselves, but in the power and the weapons God has provided us.

The Loinbelt of Truth Is Our Most Important Weapon

After instructing us to stand confidently, Paul begins to list each piece of spiritual armor. He said, "Stand therefore, having your loins girt about with truth..." (Ephesians 6:14). We saw in our last lesson that the soldier's loinbelt was the most important piece of weaponry. It held all the other pieces of armor in place. For instance, the loinbelt kept the brass breastplate from flapping around when a soldier rushed into battle. Likewise, the loinbelt provided a clip for the soldier's massive shield to rest on when it was not in use, and his sword was attached to another clip on the other side. On the back of the loinbelt, there was a pouch where he kept his lances. Thus, the loinbelt was not optional but mandatory. Without it, the soldier's armor would have literally fallen apart.

Similarly, the loinbelt of truth — which is the written Word of God — is the most important piece of spiritual weaponry we have. It is central to everything and holds all the other pieces of weaponry firmly in place. Colossians 3:16 says, "Let the word of Christ dwell in you richly in all wisdom...." When we welcome God's Word daily in our hearing and our thinking, it will produce peace (our shoes) and provide an understanding of our salvation (our helmet). It will also give us a sense of righteousness (our breastplate), strengthen our faith (our shield), and sharpen the sword of the Spirit. If we want to function victoriously as believers, we must allow the Word of God to have an active and central role in our lives.

Shoes of Peace Give Us Firm Footing

When we come to Ephesians 6:15, Paul reveals another piece of our spiritual weaponry. He says, to "...[Have] your feet shod with the preparation of the gospel of peace." The word "shod" is a form of the Greek word *hupodeo*, which is a compound of the words *hupo* and *deo*. The word *hupo* means *under*, and *deo* means *to bind*. When these words are compounded, the new word *hupodeo* means *to bind something tightly on the bottom of one's feet*, which is exactly what a Roman soldier did with his shoes.

The soldier's shoes were uniquely made of two parts: the shoe itself and the greave. The shoe portion was made of thick leather that was tightly bound around his feet. He couldn't have loose-fitting shoes because they would impair his ability to move quickly and advance in battle. Similarly, when the peace of God is tightly wrapped around our mind and emotions, we are equipped to move quickly and are ready for action.

Next, notice the verse says our feet are to be bound tightly with "...the preparation of the gospel of peace" (Ephesians 6:15). The word "preparation" is the Greek word *etoimasia*, which carries the idea of *readiness for movement*. Used here in connection with Roman soldiers, this word portrays men of war who had their shoes tied on very tightly, and hence, had a *firm footing*. With the assurance that their shoes were going to stay in place, they were ready to march out onto the battlefield and confront the enemy. Paul chose this word to denote the action of peace in our lives. He is clearly telling us that *when peace is foundational, we have a firm footing*. Peace gives us a foundation so secure that we can step out in confident faith without being moved by what we see or what we hear.

This brings us to the word "peace," which is the Greek word *eirene*, meaning *the cessation of war*. It describes *a calm, inner stability that results in the ability to conduct oneself peacefully even in the midst of circumstances that would normally be traumatic or upsetting*. This word *eirene* is the Greek equivalent for the Hebrew word *shalom*, and it expresses the idea of *wholeness, completeness or tranquility in the soul that is unaffected by outward circumstances or pressures*. God's plan is that this prevailing and conquering peace will dominate your life. Regardless of how hard the enemy or the daily affairs of life hit you, this prevailing and conquering peace will hold you in place!

There Are Two Kinds of Peace

In Scripture, there are actually two kinds of peace. First, there is peace *with* God, which is what a person experiences when he or she first comes to the Lord for salvation (*see* Romans 5:1). Peace *with* God is a spiritual condition that belongs to all believers. It comes into being the moment a person gets saved and the barrier between that person and God dissolves and his or her alienated mind comes into harmony with God.

Many Christians are at peace *with* God by virtue of their conversion experience, but they are not walking in the peace *of* God, which is a prevailing, conquering peace that surpasses natural understanding. Instead of being dominated by this protective peace of God, these individuals walk in constant fretfulness, anxiety, worry, and all kinds of other turmoil.

When you're walking in the peace *of* God, the enemy's assaults lose their power to harm you. It's as if you are in a divine bubble that protects you from everything that is happening around you. With the peace of God operating in your life, you have a conquering force that is so strong and effective, all the chaos you formerly experienced will be replaced with a peace that prevails in every area of your life.

The Soldier's 'Greaves' Provided Protection

Remember, the Roman soldier's shoes consisted of two parts: the *shoe* itself and the *greave*. The *greave* began at the top of the knee and extended down past the lower leg, all the way to the upper portion of the foot, and it was made of solid bronze or brass. It was the *greave* that protected the soldier's legs from being bruised, lacerated, or broken in battle.

At times, commanding officers gave orders that required Roman soldiers to carry out difficult and dangerous missions that forced the soldiers to walk through thorny or rocky places and to scale difficult barriers. A bruised leg meant he would probably be impaired in his fighting and in his ability to swiftly respond to an attack. Likewise, a lacerated leg from thorns meant he could potentially lose large amounts of blood and become too weakened to fight.

But because soldiers had *greaves* of brass tightly bound around their legs, they could walk through the rockiest and roughest of places without getting one scrape or bruise! Their *greaves* also protected their legs from getting shredded or suffering serious damage by fearsome thorns. Their legs were completely covered and carefully protected by their *greaves* of brass that had been wrapped around them. A soldier's *greaves* also protected him from being kicked in the shins and having his legs broken by the enemy.

What do these *greaves* mean to you as a believer? Spiritually speaking, the *greaves* are a part of your *shoes of peace*. When the prevailing, conquering peace of God is ruling in your life, you can walk through those thorny places without receiving one poisonous prick to your mind and emotions! Likewise, when the peace of God is ruling in your heart, mind, and emotions, you can forge your way through the rockiest of situations and never get one scrape or bruise. When God's peace is active in your life, it surpasses all natural understanding in its ability to protect, guard, keep, and defend you from the enemy's attacks.

The Spiked Shoes Are An Offensive and Defensive Weapon

The second part of the soldier's shoes was the thick leather bottoms that were tightly wrapped around the soldier's feet. Protruding from the underside of the shoes were extremely dangerous spikes that were one to three inches in length. These were called hobnails, and they served the soldier in two very important ways. First, these spikes helped to hold the soldier's footing in place. When a soldier had spikes on the bottom of his feet and those spikes were firmly planted into the earth, that soldier became very difficult to knock over or to move!

Similarly, when the supernatural peace of God is operative in your life, it puts spikes on the bottom of your feet that hold you firmly in place. His peace is a *keeping peace*. It will enable you to say, "Regardless of what I see or what I hear, I'm not moving! I don't care how hard it becomes, the peace of God keeps me here, and I'm not moving until the work of God in this area of my life is finished." Just as the roots of a tree hold the tree in place when strong winds come against it, God's peace, firmly fixed to the bottom of your feet, will hold you in your position of faith.

In addition to a *keeping peace*, the peace of God is also an *offensive* weapon. The apostle Paul gives us a vivid picture of how this works in Romans 16:20, which says, "And the God of peace shall bruise Satan under your feet shortly...." The word "bruise" here is the Greek word *suntribo*, and it denotes *the act of smashing and utterly crushing grapes into wine*. It also depicts *the act of snapping, breaking, and crushing bones*. In fact, it pictures breaking bones so terribly that they can never be mended or healed. These are bones that have been utterly smashed and crushed beyond recognition.

This verse pinpoints Satan's only rightful position in our lives, which is *under our feet*. Your God-given mission is to reinforce the victory Christ already won and to demonstrate just how miserably defeated Satan already is! Your healing, your miracle, your financial blessing — all of these are already yours! Jesus accomplished a total, complete, and perfect work on the Cross of Calvary and in His resurrection from the dead!

Again, the Bible declares that "...the God of peace shall bruise Satan under your feet shortly..." (Romans 16:20). The word "shortly" in this verse is also very important. It is a military term that depicts *a large group of Roman soldiers marching down a street, taking very hard, short, heavy steps when they marched in formation*. This is how these ancient men of war were taught to march. Therefore, when a large group of Roman soldiers came marching through town, their noise could be heard everywhere as they stomped and pounded the cobblestone and marble pavement in the streets. They were told to stop for no one. If someone foolishly got in their way, they were instructed to keep marching — all the while stomping and pounding their heavy feet and spikes upon the pavement.

In Romans 16:20, Paul used this same illustration to portray our victorious position in Jesus Christ. By using the word "shortly," which depicted the stomping and pounding and the short, heavy steps that Roman soldiers took, Paul gave us an extremely graphic picture! He was saying, "If the devil wants to stand in front of you and try to oppose you and the work of God in your life, then don't stop and ask him to move! Just keep marching! Keep stomping and pounding as you move forward to obey the plan of God for your life — and as you move forward in faith, do as much damage to the enemy as you possibly can!"

You Have a Shield of Faith That Covers You from Head to Toe

When we come to Ephesians 6:16, we find the fourth piece of armor we've been given. Writing under the inspiration of the Holy Spirit, Paul said, "Above all, taking the shield of faith, wherewith ye shall be able to quench all the fiery darts of the wicked."

The word "shield" here is the Greek word *thureos*, and it described *an oblong shield in the shape of a door* that was wide in width and long in length. Rather than depict the small, round decorative shields that soldiers marched with in parades, this word *thureos* depicts battle shields that were very heavy, large, and shaped like a door, just like the door of a house.

Paul's use of this word tells us that God has given us enough faith to make certain we are completely covered — just like a battle shield completely covered a Roman soldier! The moment you got saved, God gave you a specific "measure of faith" (*see* Romans 12:3). Don't ever worry or fret that God has given others more faith than He has given you. Rest assured in the fact that He has imparted enough faith to you to make sure you are covered from head to toe! Like a wide, long shield, the faith God has given you is adequate to cover every need that could ever arise in your life.

A soldier's shield was composed of multiple layers — usually six layers — of thick animal hide that had been tightly woven together. These layers of animal hide were specially tanned and then woven together so tightly that they became almost as strong as steel. Because the shield of the Roman soldier was made from all these layers of animal hides, it was extremely strong and exceptionally long-lasting and hard-wearing. Similarly, your faith is extremely tough and exceptionally durable — more so than you have ever realized! No matter how hard and how long the enemy beats against your faith, your faith can outlast his attack.

Regular Care Is Required To Keep Your Shield in Top-Notch Shape

Although the six layers of animal hide made the shield extremely strong and durable, the leather could become stiff and breakable over a period of time if it wasn't properly taken care of. So it was necessary for a soldier to take care of his shield. Each morning when he woke up, he would reach for his shield and for a small vial of oil. After saturating a piece of cloth with this heavy ointment, he would thoroughly rub the oil into the leather of the shield to keep it soft, supple, and pliable. For a soldier to ignore this daily application of oil, and to let his shield go without this kind of required care, was essentially the equivalent of his inviting certain death.

Because the shield is representative of our faith, this analogy tells us that our faith requires frequent anointings of the Holy Spirit. Without a fresh touch of the Holy Spirit's power on your life, your faith will become hard, stiff, and brittle. Faith that is ignored will almost certainly break and fall to pieces during a confrontation with the enemy. Many believers make the incredibly tragic mistake of thinking they can keep moving forward in their Christian walk on the steam of their past experiences with the Lord. Regardless of how great your past experiences and victories are, if you stop developing your faith or fail to keep your faith freshly anointed by the Holy Spirit's presence, your shield of faith is in a hazardous position. Be proactive and assume that your faith always needs a fresh anointing. By taking this approach, you will always seek to do what is necessary to keep your faith alive, active, and well!

There is something else that a soldier would do just before going into battle. He would take his shield and place it in a tub of water, allowing it to soak in the water until his shield was completely saturated. The reason soldiers did this was to be able to put out the flaming arrows that the enemy shot at them. Having a water-saturated shield gave the soldier the upper hand in battle. When those dangerous flaming arrows hit the shield, the wet surface would extinguish them on impact!

Therefore, along with allowing the Holy Spirit to freshly anoint your life on a daily basis, you also need to soak your faith in the water of the Word daily. Word-saturated faith will always extinguish the devil's fiery attacks!

If You've Laid Down Your Faith, It's Not Too Late To Pick It Up Again!

Looking once more at Ephesians 6:16, it says "Above all, taking the shield of faith, wherewith ye shall be able to quench all the fiery darts of the wicked." The words "above all" in Greek actually describe the position of faith in our lives. It means *out in front of* or *covering all.* The word "taking" in this verse is the Greek word *analambano*, which means *to pick something back up again* or *to lift back up into its correct position*. By using this word, Paul is letting us know that our shield of faith can be picked up or it can be laid down. And if we've laid down our faith at some point along the way — it is not too late for us to "pick up" our shield and walk in faith again!

Friend, going into battle against the enemy without your shield of faith is not an option. Only with your shield "...shall [you] be able to quench all the fiery darts of the wicked" (Ephesians 6:16). The phrase "shall be able" is the Greek word *dunamai*, which is from the word *dunamis*, and it means *powerful, able,* or *supernaturally enabled.* The use of this word tells us that when you hold your shield of faith in front of you — and when that shield of faith is both anointed by the Holy Spirit and saturated with the Word of God — your faith positions you to move in God's explosive and dynamic power!

In our next lesson, we will take a close look at the remaining three pieces of weaponry: the helmet of salvation, the sword of the Spirit, and the lance of prayer.

STUDY QUESTIONS

Study to shew thyself approved unto God, a workman that needeth not to be ashamed, rightly dividing the word of truth.
— 2 Timothy 2:15

1. What interesting new insights did you discover about the *shoes of peace*? How about the *shield of faith*? How does this teaching help you better understand the purpose and practical use of these pieces of weaponry?
2. As a believer, you have experienced peace *with* God. But are you experiencing the peace *of* God — a prevailing, conquering peace that cannot be figured out by the human mind?
3. According to John 14:27 and Ephesians 2:14, *where* does this kind of peace come from? What do Isaiah 26:3 and Philippians 4:6-8 say you need to do to experience this peace?
4. To have a strong, robust shield of faith, you need the Holy Spirit to freshly anoint your life on a daily basis, and you also need to soak your faith in the water of the Word. What reason do these passages repeatedly provide for investing time soaking in God's Word?
   - Numbers 23:19
   - 1 Kings 8:56

- Psalm 12:6 and 119:89
- Ezekiel 12:25
- Luke 21:33

PRACTICAL APPLICATION

But be ye doers of the word, and not hearers only, deceiving your own selves.
— James 1:22

1. Can you recall a situation in which the peace of God functioned as a Roman soldier's *shoes* in your life — grounding you securely in your place and protecting you as you walked through rocky or thorny circumstances? If so, briefly share what happened.
2. One of the greatest blessings of the supernatural peace of God operating in your life is that it puts spikes on the bottom of your feet that hold you firmly in place, regardless of what is happening. What challenge are you currently facing in which you desperately need the supernatural peace of God? Take this situation to the Lord in prayer and ask Him to fill you with His divine peace (*see* Philippians 4:6,7).
3. Just as a Roman soldier's shield needed a daily application of oil to keep it soft and pliable, your faith requires frequent anointings of the Holy Spirit to keep it from becoming hard, stiff, and brittle. How would you describe the condition of your faith? Does it stand up or fall apart in times of battle? What specific steps can you take to *recharge*, *reenergize*, and *reposition* your faith out in front of your life again?
4. When was the last time you received a fresh anointing of the Holy Spirit? If you'd like a brand-new infilling of the Holy Spirit's power, pray and ask Him to touch you right now!

TOPIC

The Helmet of Salvation, Sword of the Spirit, Lance of Prayer

SCRIPTURES

1. **Ephesians 6:17,18** — And take the helmet of salvation, and the sword of the Spirit, which is the word of God: praying always with all prayer and supplication in the Spirit, and watching thereunto with all perseverance and supplication for all saints.

GREEK WORDS

1. "helmet" — **περικεφαλαία** (*perikephalaia*): compound of **περι** (*peri*) and **κεφαλή** (*kephale*); the word **περι** (*peri*) means around, and **κεφαλή** (*kephale*) means the head; compounded together, denotes a piece of armor that fits very tightly around the head
2. "salvation" — **σωτήριος** (*soterios*): saved or delivered; in the broadest sense of the word, it means to be brought into a safe place; saved, delivered from danger, healed, restored, rescued
3. "take" — **δέχομαι** (*dechomai*): receive in a welcoming way; receive what is offered; a willing attitude to accept
4. "sword" — **μάχαιρα** (*machaira*): a sword approximately 19 inches long, with both sides being razor sharp; this two-edged sword inflicted a wound far worse than other swords
5. "word" — **ῥῆμα** (*rhema*): a word spoken clearly; spoken vividly; spoken in undeniable language; a word spoken in unmistakable, unquestionable, certain, and definite terms; in the New Testament, the word **ῥῆμα** (*rhema*) carries the idea of a quickened word
6. "with all prayer" — **διὰ πάσης προσευχῆς** (*dia pases proseuches*): with all kinds of prayer

SYNOPSIS

We have noted in our previous lessons that deep inside the Kremlin in the city of Moscow there is a fabulous collection of weapons on display in what is called the Armory Museum. What's interesting is that in this museum there are also a number of royal thrones as well as several royal crowns of former Russian czars. There is even a section which features the lavish jewelry that was worn by the horses that were used in the service of the czars and their families.

Of course there is also a splendid assortment of sabers, swords, shields, and arrows covered in turquoise, rubies, emeralds, and diamonds — some made of 24 karat gold! And yet, as resplendent as these weapons are, their magnificence is dwarfed in comparison by the spiritual armor God has given us. The apostle Paul describes our divine weaponry in Ephesians 6:14-18, and in this lesson, we are going to set our gaze on the helmet of salvation, the sword of the Spirit, and the lance of prayer.

The emphasis of this lesson:

Three additional weapons God has given us are the helmet of salvation, which is walking in the full knowledge of our salvation; the sword of the Spirit, which is a clear word of scripture given by the Holy Spirit to lethally stab the enemy; and the lance of prayer, which includes all kinds of prayers that enable us to deal a death blow to the devil before he gets too close.

A Review of Ephesians 6:13-16

Writing under the inspiration of the Holy Spirit, the apostle Paul said, "Wherefore take unto you the whole armour of God, that ye may be able to withstand in the evil day, and having done all, to stand" (Ephesians 6:13). In this verse, the phrase "whole armour" in Greek is the word *panoplia*, and it pictures *a Roman soldier fully dressed in his armor from head to toe.* His full attire and weaponry consisted of seven pieces of armor: the loinbelt, breastplate, shoes, shield, helmet, sword, and lance.

When you receive God's power and are dressed in all of the weapons He provides, suddenly you become a walloping, conquering force! He enables you to "withstand in the evil day." We've seen that the word "withstand" in Greek is *antistenai*, which means *to stand against*; *to push against*; or *to aggressively position oneself against.* It is a picture of a soldier that is moving forward to drive back the forces of darkness in the "evil day."

This verse tells us that when you're filled with the power of God and dressed in His armor, you're no longer running from the devil. Instead, you're pursuing him and putting him on the run! You become filled with the full force of Heaven's army, and its might is released through you. Like a divine force of nature, you turn into God's hurricane, tornado, or earthquake that shakes up and pushes back the domain of darkness.

Paul went on to say, "Stand therefore, having your loins girt about with truth, and having on the breastplate of righteousness" (Ephesians 6:14). In this verse, the word "stand" is the Greek word *stete*, which means *to stand upright*. It pictures *a Roman soldier who confidently stands with his head held high and his shoulders thrown back*. This lets us know that when we're equipped in the whole armor of God — which includes the loinbelt of truth and the breastplate of righteousness — we have every reason to stand up straight and be confident in God! We can hold our head high, throw our shoulders back, and be assured and confident in the power and the weapons He has provided us.

When we come to Ephesians 6:15, we are instructed to have our "…feet shod with the preparation of the gospel of peace." And in verse 16, Paul said, "Above all, taking the shield of faith, wherewith ye shall be able to quench all the fiery darts of the wicked." In the original text, the words "above all" is the Greek phrase *epi pasin*, which means "*Out in front of all…*" or "*Covering all….*" This describes the position of our faith, which is supposed to be aggressively *out front* where it can *completely cover* us and protect us from all harm.

We also saw that the word "taking" in this verse is the Greek word *analambano*, which means *to pick something back up again* or *to lift back up into its correct position*. Here, Paul is telling us that our shield of faith can be picked up or it can be laid down. And if we've laid down our faith at some point for some reason, we can "pick it up again" and begin walking in faith!

It is with our shield of faith out in front of us that we are "…able to quench all the fiery darts of the wicked" (Ephesians 6:16). The words "fiery darts" are from the Greek word *belos*, which described *an arrow with its tip wrapped with fabric soaked in flammable liquid so that it would burn with hot flames*. This word *belos* was used by the famous Greek writer Thucydides to depict arrows that were hollow inside and filled with combustible fluids that, upon impact, exploded into a blazing fire. The Bible calls these "fiery darts of the wicked."

The word "wicked" is the Greek word *poneros*, and it describes *something malicious or malignant*; *something foul, vile, hostile, and vicious*. When the enemy shoots his arrows at us, they are often *savage*, *wild*, and *vicious*, and when they explode, they set our human passions aflame. It is only when our shield of faith has been regularly anointed by the Holy Spirit and soaked in God's Word that those fiery darts will be extinguished. The oil of the Spirit and the water of the Word preserve and empower your faith to function at full force, guaranteeing the enemy's fiery darts will have little to no effect.

God Has Given Us the 'Helmet of Salvation' To Guard and Protect Our Mind

The next piece of armor Paul names provides supernatural protection for our mind, which is the control center of our life. In Ephesians 6:17, Paul said, "And take the helmet of salvation…." The word "helmet" is the Greek word *perikephalaia*. It is a compound of the word *peri*, which means *around*, and the word *kephale*, which is the word for *the head*. When these words are compounded together, it denotes *a piece of armor that fits very tightly around the head.*

Of all the pieces of a soldier's armor, the loinbelt was most important because it held everything together; the breastplate was the most brilliant and glorious; and the helmet was the most noticeable. When a Roman soldier walked down the street with his helmet on, the brightly colored plume of horse hair spouting from his helmet would stand out in any crowd. You couldn't help but notice it.

Similarly, the most noticeable gift God has given you is salvation through Christ. It is the most intricate, elaborate, and priceless transformation He has mercifully and graciously brought about in your life, and when you're walking in the powerful reality of all that your salvation means to you, it is visible to others. Paul said the gift of our salvation is like a helmet.

The helmet of a Roman soldier: This piece of armor was made of bronze and very heavy. In fact, it was so heavy that the interior of the helmet was lined with a spongy material in order to soften its weight upon the soldier's head. This helmet actually wrapped around the whole head and was equipped with pieces of armor that were specifically designed to protect the cheeks and jaws. It even extended down the back of the neck to protect the back of the head. This piece of armor was so strong, so massive, and so heavy that nothing could pierce it — not even a hammer or a battle axe. If the Roman soldier didn't have his helmet on when he went out to fight, he could be absolutely certain that he would lose his head.

Similarly, your salvation is like a helmet that protects your mind. That is what the devil (*diablos*) is after. He builds a road that is headed straight for your head in order to penetrate your thinking and take you captive by his deceptions. If your salvation — like a helmet — is not worn tightly around your mind, the enemy will come to chop away the multiple benefits and blessings of your salvation right out of your belief system. He will whack away at your spiritual foundation, trying to tell you that healing, deliverance, preservation of mind, and soundness are not really a part of Jesus' redemptive work on the Cross. By the time the enemy is finished with your mind, the only thing he will leave you with is Heaven!

It is vital we study God's Word and make it a goal to understand and walk in the full knowledge of our salvation. We need to know what the Bible says about healing, about deliverance from demonic powers, about spiritual authority over the devil, and all that we have inherited through the gift of our redemption. When our minds are trained and taught to think correctly in terms of our salvation, that knowledge becomes a protective helmet in our lives!

What does the word "salvation" mean? The word "salvation" is the Greek word *soterios*, which means *saved* or *delivered*. In the broadest sense of the word, it means *to be brought into a safe place*. Moreover, it means *to be saved, delivered from danger, brought into a safe place, healed, restored,* or *rescued*. When we carefully look at the meaning of this word *soterios* — translated here as "salvation" — it is not referring to our life in Heaven. We won't need to be healed, rescued, or delivered from danger in Heaven. These are the benefits we need in this life right now.

Paul said we are to "…take the helmet of salvation…" (Ephesians 6:17). This word "take" is the Greek word *dechomai*, which means *to receive in a welcoming way* or *to receive what is offered*. It is *a willing attitude to accept something*. In this case, God is offering us the helmet of salvation, but He is not going to force us to take it. In order to receive the renewed mind He is offering, we have to be actively involved, reading and studying the Bible to learn what it says about our salvation and Jesus' redemptive work to deliver, heal, preserve, and give us a sound mind. As you faithfully meditate on the Word of God, salvation will become so real to you — you will become so convinced of your salvation and of all its benefits — that your mind will be able to rest securely in God, no longer capable of being penetrated by doubt and unbelief.

God Has Placed a Razor-sharp Sword in Our Hands

In addition to the helmet of salvation, Ephesians 6:17 tells us to "…[take] the sword of the Spirit, which is the word of God." The word "sword" here is the Greek word *machaira*, and it described *a sword approximately 19 inches long, with both sides being razor sharp*. This two-edged sword inflicted a wound far worse than other swords, and the sight of it brought fear to people's minds.

Very often the tip of this sword was turned upward and sometimes even twisted like a corkscrew. Because of its razor-sharpness, it could easily be thrust into the abdomen of an adversary, and by a simple twisting of the sword while it was inserted, the attacker would spill the victim's entrails on the ground. All of this meaning is packed within the Greek word *machaira* — translated here as "sword." Spiritually speaking, God has given you a razor-sharp sword that strikes fear into the heart of demons and can deliver a deadly blow.

And notice it is "…the sword of the Spirit, which is the word of God" (Ephesians 6:17). We have already seen that the loinbelt of truth is the *written* Word of God, but this facet of God's Word is different. In this verse, the term "word" is the Greek word *rhema*, and it describes *a word spoken clearly*; *spoken vividly*; or *spoken in undeniable language*. It denotes *a word spoken in unmistakable, unquestionable, certain, and definite terms*. In the New Testament, the word *rhema* carries the idea of a quickened word — something in the Scriptures that suddenly comes alive. And when that word comes alive, it places razor-sharp sword-power in the palm of your hands!

A perfect example of the sword of the Spirit in action is when Jesus was in the wilderness being tempted by the devil. This account is documented in Matthew 4 and Luke 4. For 40 days and 40 nights, Jesus was intensely tested by Satan, and at the end of that time period — when Jesus was at His weakest point — Satan struck with a vengeance. Because this testing of the devil was so extreme and intense, the Lord Jesus needed a *rhema* — a "sword of the Spirit" — to withstand the attacks.

Jesus faced the enemy in the same way we face the enemy in life, and He gave us an example of how we are to answer Satan. Every time Satan hurled his lies and tried to pressure Jesus, over and over, Jesus said, **"It is written...."** The Holy Spirit, in all of His power and might, provided a specific verse in due season! He drew a scripture out of that reservoir of Scripture stored up inside of Jesus' spirit and quickened one of those verses to His mind. Jesus then *spoke* it with great power and authority. He wielded that *rhema* word like a mighty blade — and the enemy could not stand against it! The Word of God in Jesus' mouth became a deadly sword that He stabbed the enemy with again and again.

When you're in a difficult place, the Holy Spirit will reach into the Word of God that is stored inside your spirit and give you the perfect verse you need in that moment. Sometimes He will cause the Bible verse you are reading to leap off the page and come alive in your heart. That verse is the answer you need! It is the *rhema* sword of the Spirit that will inflict a deadly blow to the enemy as it comes out of your mouth. Indeed, the Scripture itself is filled with every *rhema* word you will ever need, which is why the loinbelt of truth is so important. Remember, the sword hung on a clip on the side of the loinbelt, which symbolizes the Bible. As long as the Word is wrapped tightly around you, you will have access to any word the Spirit will give you. It will become a sword for you, and be exactly what you need to put the devil on the run!

The Lance of Prayer

The last piece of weaponry in the Roman soldier's arsenal was his *lance.* Although the word "lance" is not specifically written in the passage, it is definitely alluded to in Ephesians 6:18, which says, "Praying always with all prayer and supplication in the Spirit, and watching thereunto with all perseverance and supplication for all saints."

The lances used by the large and diverse Roman army varied greatly in size, shape, and length. Over the course of many centuries, these various lances had been modified substantially, so the Roman soldier had all kinds of lances at his disposal. The old Greek lances used during Homer's time were normally made of ash wood and were about six to seven feet long with a solid iron lance-head at the end.

Like the lance itself, the iron head of the lance varied tremendously in form. Often it resembled a leaf, a bulrush, a sharp barb, or simply a jagged point like the lance-heads used on spears today. Some lances were small; others were extremely long. Most Roman soldiers carried both lances, short and long. The smaller, shorter lances were used for gouging and thrusting at an enemy up close, whereas the longer lances were used for hurling at an enemy from a distance.

The Roman army used a lance called the pilum, which was about six feet long and primarily used for throwing at an enemy from a distance. These pilum lances were used when an opposing force came to attack the Romans' fortified position or encampment. Rather than wait for the enemy to come upon them and suffer many losses, the Roman soldiers would hurl these extremely heavy lances through the air toward their foes. By doing this, the Romans could strike many of the enemy soldiers to the ground before they were able to penetrate their army encampment.

What does all of this have to do with spiritual armor?

The apostle Paul instructed us to put on the "whole armor" — *panoplia* — of God, which was all the armor of a Roman soldier. This weaponry would have included the lance, which came in various shapes, sizes, and lengths. As Paul comes to the weapon of prayer, he is imagining this variety of lances and spears. Now by revelation, he begins to compare these various lances to the various kinds of prayer that God has made available to us.

This is why Paul said, "Praying always, with all prayer and supplication..." (Ephesians 6:18). The phrase "with all prayer" in Greek literally means *with all kinds of prayer*. Just as Roman soldiers used all different types of lances in battle, Paul tells us that God has made many kinds of prayer available to us for different moments in our fight of faith.

Like a lance loaded with deadly weight, intercession can deal a wound so fatal to the domain of darkness that it hinders the devil's lethal devices from becoming a reality in others' lives or in our own lives, families, businesses, churches, and ministries. God is so good to us that He has provided us the ability to attack the enemy from a distance, which means if we will use the weapon of prayer properly, we can stop the enemy's attack before he gets near.

Thus, the phrase "with all prayer" in Ephesians 6:18 can be translated:

"Pray with all manner of prayer"

"Pray with all kinds of prayer"

"Pray with all the kinds of prayers that are available for you to use"

In our final lesson, we will turn our attention to Second Corinthians 10:4 and 5 and see what God says about using our spiritual weaponry to destroy what the Bible calls "strongholds" in our lives.

STUDY QUESTIONS

Study to shew thyself approved unto God, a workman that needeth not to be ashamed, rightly dividing the word of truth.
— 2 Timothy 2:15

1. What fascinating new facts did you see about the *helmet of salvation*? How about the *sword of the Spirit* and the *lance of prayer*? How do these truths help you better understand and make the most of these pieces of weaponry?
2. Jesus' time of testing in the wilderness is a great picture of what it looks like to wield the sword of the Spirit. Carefully read through Matthew 4:1-11 (*also* Luke 4:1-13). What patterns stand out to you in Satan's attacks and Jesus' response? Has the enemy ever tried to get you to meet a healthy need (i.e. bread to eat) in an unhealthy way? Has the enemy ever twisted God's Word to get you to believe his lies? If so, which scriptures did he use? How did it affect you?
3. God instructs us to "Pray at all times (on every occasion, in every season) in the Spirit, with all [manner of] prayer..." (Ephesians 6:18 *AMPC*). Three of the most common types of prayer in Scripture are prayers of *consecration*, *petition*, and *thanksgiving*. Consider the examples below, and describe how you would apply each kind of prayer in your own life right now.
   - *Prayer of Consecration*: 1 Samuel 1:11; 2 Samuel 23:16
   - *Prayer of Petition*: James 5:17,18; Matthew 6:5,6
   - *Prayer of Thanksgiving*: Ephesians 1:16; 1 Thessalonians 1:2; 2 Thessalonians 1:3

PRACTICAL APPLICATION

But be ye doers of the word, and not hearers only, deceiving your own selves.
—James 1:22

1. Have you ever been talking with someone and just had a strong gut-feeling that they were a fellow believer? How was it confirmed? What was it about them that stood out? Have you ever had a total stranger ask you if *you* were a Christian? What was it about you that they noticed?
2. Have you ever experienced the "sword of the Spirit" before? Has the Holy Spirit ever reminded you of a verse you had studied before that helped you in a time of need? Which scripture(s) did He recall to your mind? What were the results of you believing and speaking His Word?
3. How much do you actually know about what you have received through your salvation in Christ? Why not decide today to become a lifelong student of God's Word? We encourage you to really begin to study what the Bible says about your healing, your deliverance, your authority over the devil, and what it means to be a joint heir with Jesus. As you learn about the blessings of your redemption, it will protect your mind from the enemy's attacks.

LESSON 10

TOPIC

Pulling Down Strongholds

SCRIPTURES

1. **2 Corinthians 10:4,5** — (For the weapons of our warfare are not carnal, but mighty through God to the pulling down of strong holds;) Casting down imaginations, and every high thing that exalteth itself against the knowledge of God…."

GREEK WORDS

1. "weapons" — **ὅπλα** (*hopla*): from **ὅπλον** (*hoplon*), armor, weapons; used in Ephesians 6:14-18 to depict the whole armor of God that potentially belongs to every believer
2. "warfare" — **στρατεία** (*strateia*): a well-planned attack; derived from **στρατεύομαι** (*strateuomai*), which depicts strategic warfare; methods

to be used in an attack and the route chosen to carry out a debilitating assault

3. "carnal"— **σαρκικός** (*sarkikos*): fleshly; natural; whatever is derived from the fleshly, natural, or material world
4. "mighty"— **δυνατὰ** (*dunata*): from **δύναμις** (*dunamis*), power; pictures explosive, superhuman power that comes with enormous energy and produces phenomenal, extraordinary, and unparalleled results; used to depict the full might and power of an advancing army
5. "through God"— **τῷ Θεῷ** (*to Theo*): through God; through the instrumentality of God; through a partnership with God
6. "pulling down"— **καθαιρέω** (*kathaireo*): to take down; to disassemble, if needed, bit by bit; to demolish; to destroy; to dismantle; to throw down; to knock down, break up, pull apart, and take to pieces until nothing is left standing; used to picture pulling down the walls of a well-defended fortress
7. "strongholds"— **ὀχύρωμα** (*ochuroma*): fortress; castle; citadel; pictures a stronghold with walls fortified to keep outsiders on the outside; a dreadful prison constructed deep inside a fortress that was intended to prevent a hostage or prisoner from escaping; a place of arrest, captivity, confinement, detention, imprisonment, or incarceration
8. "casting down"— **καθαιρέω** (*kathaireo*): to take down; to disassemble, if needed, bit by bit; to demolish; to destroy; to dismantle; to throw down; to knock down, break up, pull apart, and take to pieces until nothing is left standing; used to picture pulling down the walls of a well-defended fortress
9. "imaginations"— **λογισμός** (*logismos*): where we get the word logic; used to denote thoughts or reasoning in the mind
10. "every"— **πᾶν** (*pan*): all; an all-encompassing word, nothing excluded
11. "high thing"— **ὕψωμα** (*hupsoma*): barrier; bulwark; presumption
12. "exalted itself"— **ἐπαίρω** (*epairo*): to lift up; depicts a haughty, arrogant, prideful rising; to wrongfully assert
13. "against the knowledge of God"— **κατὰ τῆς γνώσεως τοῦ Θεοῦ** (*kata tes gnoseos tou Theou*) the word **κατά** (*kata*) means against; in this phrase, it means to dominate, quash, pull under its control, or to subdue; the words **τῆς γνώσεως τοῦ Θεοῦ** (*tes gnoseos tou Theou*) depict knowledge that finds its origin in God or absolutely clear knowledge that comes from God; hence, this phrase depicts a war against all knowledge that comes from God

SYNOPSIS

Situated near the banks of the Neva River is the Peter and Paul Fortress, whose foundation was first laid in 1703. Its walls are thick as well as high, and its purpose was to defend the city of Saint Petersburg. As most fortifications, it was constructed to keep outsiders on the outside and, if needed, to keep prisoners on the inside. That's what a fortress — or *stronghold* — was intended to do.

What is true in the natural realm is also true in the realm of the spirit. There are people living today who have impregnable walls or fortresses in their souls. They are trapped as prisoners by their own vain imaginations. Little by little, over an extended period of time, Satan deceives people into accepting his lies about themselves, about God, and about life in order to erect a stronghold in their soul.

Thankfully, anyone that is incarcerated by the enemy's lies can break free — including you! You can learn how to recognize strongholds and pull them down by employing the powerful spiritual weapons God has given you!

The emphasis of this lesson:

Along with the supernatural weapons, God gives us supernatural strategies to pull down and destroy strongholds, which is any lie we are believing that is imprisoning us. Through the power of the Holy Spirit and the use of our spiritual weaponry, we are to cast down every imagination and thought — logical or illogical — that tries to supersede God's Word.

The Most Important Part of Spiritual Warfare

The mind has the ability to dream up wild, unfounded, unbiblical ideas about the devil and our warfare against him. If we do not have a solid biblical understanding of the devil and our Christ-imparted authority over him, along with our divinely empowered weaponry to be used against him, we're left wide open to all kinds of wrong thinking, vain imaginations, fears, and unfounded methods of opposing the devil.

To be clear, not all teaching about spiritual warfare is bad. In fact, some is exceptionally good. But as we approach this topic, we must guard against superstitious, homemade remedies about spiritual warfare. It is our responsibility to base our teachings and actions firmly on what the Word of God has to say rather than on exciting hype that stirs the emotions or wild imaginations that temporarily thrills a frenzied crowd of believers.

It is interesting to note that of the five times the words "war" and "warfare" are used in the New Testament, they are never used once in connection with the devil. For example, both times these words are used in Second Corinthians 10:3-5, they denote *mental bondages that must be pulled down.* These are mental strongholds that the devil plants in our minds. In context, these verses refer to a person who must make an immovable decision to take charge of his mind and take captive the thoughts that the devil has planted in his head. This is the most important part of spiritual warfare.

God Gives Us Supernatural Strategies For Our Supernatural Weapons

Under the unction of the Holy Spirit, Paul wrote to the church in Corinth — and *us* — and said, "For the weapons of our warfare are not carnal, but mighty through God to the pulling down of strong holds" (2 Corinthians 10:4). The word "weapons" in this verse is the Greek word *hopla*, from the word *hoplon*, which describes *armor* or *weapons.* It is the same word used in Ephesians 6:14-18 to depict *the whole armor of God that potentially belongs to every believer.* These are the seven pieces of weaponry we've been studying in this series: the loinbelt of truth, breastplate of righteousness, shoes of peace, shield of faith, helmet of salvation, sword of the Spirit, and lance of prayer.

The word "warfare" in this verse is also important. It is the Greek word *strateia*, and it describes *a well-planned attack.* It is derived from the word *strateuomai*, which depicts *strategic warfare.* It is where we get the word *strategy*, and it denotes *methods to be used in an attack and the route chosen to carry out a debilitating assault.* This word lets us know that in addition to God giving us weaponry, He will also give us *divine strategy* on how to use our weapons — telling us the best route chosen to carry out a debilitating assault against our enemy.

The Bible states that the weapons and strategies God gives us are not "carnal." This word "carnal" is the Greek word *sarkikos*, meaning *fleshly* or *natural.* It depicts *whatever is derived from the fleshly, natural, or material world.* In context here, Paul is telling us there is nothing fleshly or natural about our weapons or strategies. Therefore, the strategies God gives us may not make any sense because they won't be something our brain would come up with. They are *supernatural* strategies for *supernatural* weapons.

Our Weapons Are Mighty Through God

Paul goes on to say that our weapons are "mighty through God." The word "mighty" here is the Greek word *dunata*, which is from the word *dunamis*, meaning *power*. As we have seen in our past lessons, the word *dunamis* describes *a force of nature like a tornado, a hurricane*, or *an earthquake*. It pictures *explosive, superhuman power that comes with enormous energy and produces phenomenal, extraordinary, and unparalleled results*. It is the same word used to depict *the full might and power of an advancing army*. This means, when you have the mighty — *dunamis* — power of God and His divine strategy, you are like a supernatural hurricane or tornado that shows up to blow away the enemy. It's as if all of Heaven's army has arrived to drive evil out of your territory.

But we must remember that the weapons we have are only mighty "through God." The words "through God" are translated from the Greek words *to Theo*, which means *through God*; *through the instrumentality of God*; or *through a partnership with God*. This is not us being mighty in our own ability. It is us deciding in our heart to advance and defeat the enemy, and God joining Himself to us by His Spirit, enabling us to "pull down" the strongholds in our lives.

This brings us to the phrase "pulling down," which is the Greek word *kathaireo*, and it means *to take down, to throw down*, or *to disassemble, if needed, bit by bit*. It can also be translated *to demolish*; *to destroy*; *to dismantle*; or *to knock down, break up, pull apart, and take to pieces, until nothing is left standing*. This word *kathaireo* is the term used to depict *the pulling down of the walls of a well-defended fortress*. This word pictures great determination and lets us know that if we are going to effectively "pull down" the enemy's strongholds, we have to be totally committed to attack and tear them to pieces until nothing remains.

What Is a Stronghold?

Looking once more at Second Corinthians 10:4, it says, "For the weapons of our warfare are not carnal, but mighty through God to the pulling down of *strong holds*." The Greek word for "strongholds" here is the word *ochuroma*, and it describes *a fortress, a castle*, or *a citadel*. It pictures *a stronghold with walls fortified to keep outsiders on the outside.* At the same time, it depicts *a dreadful prison constructed deep inside a fortress that was intended to prevent a hostage or prisoner from escaping.* Thus, a "stronghold" is *a place of arrest, captivity, confinement, detention, imprisonment,* or *incarceration.*

In a spiritual sense, **a stronghold is any lie you are believing that imprisons you**. The enemy is very strategic and persistent in his efforts to construct a stronghold. Little by little, he stealthily presents you with a lie here and a deception there, again and again. Each lie you believe becomes another brick in the wall of the stronghold he is attempting to construct. Although you can't see or touch it, the imaginary prison bars are there holding you hostage to ideas and imaginations that have no basis in reality.

Once the enemy's lie has become so deeply rooted in your mind — which is the central control center of your life — from that lofty position, the devil then begins to dictate to you what you're going to think, how you are going to act, and what your future is and isn't going to be. Like a wicked tyrant, he moves in and begins to oppress and dominate your life. As a prisoner to his lie, you begin to see your entire life through the lens of that lie. You believe that lie is your reality, and when someone else who sees the truth about you comes and tries to help you, they can't seem to break through to you because you're living behind the walls of a well defended fortress — a stronghold.

We Are To 'Cast Down Imaginations'

The only way you're going to break free from a lie that holds you captive is to determine to pull it down. This is why the apostle Paul tells us that our job as believers includes, "Casting down imaginations, and every high thing that exalteth itself against the knowledge of God…" (2 Corinthians 10:5).

Interestingly, the phrase "casting down" is actually the same word translated as "pulling down" in Second Corinthians 10:4. It is the Greek word *kathaireo*, and again, it means *to take down* or *to disassemble, if needed, bit by bit.* It can be translated *to demolish*; *to destroy*; *to dismantle*; *to throw down*; or *to knock down.* Moreover, it can mean *to break up, pull apart, and take to pieces until nothing is left standing.* It is used to picture pulling down the walls of a well-defended fortress.

Specifically, Paul said we are to cast down "imaginations," which is a clear indicator of the realm where the devil works — in the mind. The Greek word for "imaginations" in this verse is *logismos*, and it is where we get the word *logic*, as in *logical thinking*. It is used to denote *thoughts* or *reasoning in the mind*, and therefore identifies where the enemy's attack is taking place — in our imaginations. To be clear, a "stronghold" is anything that arrests you, confines you, or incarcerates you and keeps you from moving forward.

A stronghold can be *logical* or *illogical*.

An *illogical* stronghold is *one that is made up of unrealistic worries and fears*. An example of this would be a skinny person who consistently looks into the mirror and sees herself as fat. What she sees about herself does *not* match reality, but it is real to her. She is concerned that if she eats, she is going to get into trouble physically. Therefore, she starves herself and becomes anorexic. That is totally illogical. The truth is she is too skinny, and her health is in jeopardy. If she doesn't start eating, it's going to drastically affect her life. This is an example of an *illogical* stronghold.

In contrast, a *logical* stronghold is *one that makes sense to your mind*. For example, let's say God tells you to do something — maybe it is to begin a certain ministry, start a new business, or go back to school. In this case, a logical stronghold would be a lie that thinks, *God, I hear what You're saying, but I can't do what You're telling me to do because I don't have enough money...* or *I don't have enough education...* or *I don't have enough experience*. A *logical* stronghold will arrest you and keep you from taking a step of faith. This kind is very difficult to deal with because it is logical, and the facts get in the way. The bottom line is, if God gives us a word of instruction, we need to do what He says — period. His word overrides our logic. If you find yourself not stepping out in obedience to do what God tells you to do, you are bound by a logical stronghold.

Whether a stronghold is logical or illogical, its effects are the same. Both are a place of arrest that incarcerates its victim.

Cast Down 'Every High Thing' That Exalts Itself Against the Knowledge of God

Along with casting down imaginations, Paul instructed us to cast down "...every high thing that exalteth itself against the knowledge of God..."

(2 Corinthians 10:5). The word "every" here is the Greek word *pan*, and it is *an all-encompassing word*, indicating *all, nothing excluded.* And the words "high thing" is a translation of the Greek word *hupsoma*, which describes *a barrier, a bulwark*; or *a presumption.* Thus, anything that is blocking you from stepping forward in faith, to do what you know God has asked you to do, He wants you to cast down.

The Bible describes these barriers or presumptions as something that "…exalteth itself against the knowledge of God…." The phrase "exalteth itself" is the Greek word *epairo*, which means *to lift up*. It depicts *a haughty, arrogant, prideful rising*; it can also mean *to wrongfully assert*. Paul said this haughty, prideful attitude rises up "against the knowledge of God." In the Greek, this phrase is *kata tes gnoseos tou Theou*. The word *kata* means *against*, and in this phrase, it means *to dominate, quash, pull under its control,* or *to subdue*. The words *tes gnoseos tou Theou* depict *knowledge that finds its origin in God* or *absolutely clear knowledge that comes from God.* Hence, this phrase depicts *a war against all knowledge that comes from God.* Here is an example:

The Bible says by Jesus' "…stripes ye are healed" (1 Peter 2:24). That is knowledge that comes from God. There are people who have a stronghold in their mind that says, *Well I know the Bible says I'm healed by Jesus' stripes, but the reality is, I'm not healed. And I've been trying to be healed for a long time. I'll probably never be healed.* Did you catch that? The lie in the minds of these people is exalting itself against the knowledge of God.

Or how about this: God says in His Word that you are *the righteousness of God in Christ Jesus* (*see* 2 Corinthians 5:21). That is clear knowledge that comes from God. However, you may have a stronghold that fights against this truth. Thoughts and feelings of unworthiness in your mind lie to you, bringing condemnation, guilt, and a sense of unrighteousness. This is what the Bible calls a "high thing" — a barrier or presumption — that arrogantly "exalteth itself" and wars against the knowledge of God. It is a stronghold fighting against what God says about you.

It's Time To Make a Decision

Friend, you have to decide who and what you're going to listen to. Are you going to listen to those nagging, negative thoughts or are you going to listen to what God says about you? Who you listen to determines what you will become, because what you believe will become your reality. If you've been listening to a lie, that lie has probably already become your reality — or is in the process of *becoming* your reality. You have to shut your ears to Satan's lies and open your ears to the knowledge that comes from God's Word —the loinbelt of truth — that empowers and holds in place all the pieces of your spiritual weaponry.

If there's anything squashing the truth of God's Word — anything contrary to what Scripture says that is trying to control you or take you down — it is a stronghold and does not belong in your thinking. You do not have to be a victim any longer or be a slave to the wrong thoughts buzzing around in your brain. Just grab hold of the mighty spiritual weapons God has provided, and receive the divine strategy and strength the Holy Spirit wants to give you as you seek Him. Dressed in your spiritual armor, you *can* pull down, dismantle, or disassemble any stronghold in your life until no trace of it remains.

STUDY QUESTIONS

Study to shew thyself approved unto God, a workman that needeth not to be ashamed, rightly dividing the word of truth.
— 2 Timothy 2:15

1. Like many believers, you may be battling strongholds of *worry*, *fear*, and *condemnation*. To help you dismantle these fortresses of lies, take time to slowly soak in these promises from God's Word. Consider reading them in several different Bible versions over the next week, and when you complete the week of reflection, journal any changes you experience in your thinking as well as your level of trust in God.
   - **Wipe Out Worry**: Matthew 6:25-34; Luke 12:22-34; Philippians 4:6-8
   - **Demolish Fear**: Isaiah 41:10-14; Hebrews 13:5,6; Psalm 91; Psalm 121; Proverbs 3:24-26
   - **Crush Condemnation**: John 3:16-18; Romans 8:1,2,31-34; 1 John 3:19-21
2. Your mind is *the control center* of your life, and Jesus wants to be Lord of it. What do Romans 12:2 and Ephesians 4:22-24 say you need to do in order for Jesus to be Lord of your mind? How do you think God's instructions in Colossians 3:1-3; Isaiah 26:3; and Philippians

4:8 relate to this? What practical steps can you take to involve yourself in this highly effective spiritual practice?

PRACTICAL APPLICATION

But be ye doers of the word, and not hearers only,
deceiving your own selves.
—James 1:22

1. Are their areas in your mind and emotions that are currently being influenced or controlled by the enemy's lies? Think about areas where you find yourself repeatedly being attacked — such as issues of anger, fear, doubt, or impurity. Do you feel like a prisoner to these areas of your mind and emotions?
2. Give at least one example of a *logical* and an *illogical* stronghold that the devil has tried to establish in your life (either past or present). Which was more difficult to deal with? Why?
3. In addition to equipping you with spiritual weapons, God will also give you a *divine strategy* to defeat the devil. In what area of your life right now do you desperately need God's divine strategy to conquer the enemy? Take a moment and pray, *"Holy Spirit, please show me the specific actions I need to take to carry out a debilitating assault against Satan and effectively dismantle this stronghold. In Jesus' Name."* Be still and listen. What is God speaking to you?

Notes

Notes

Notes

Notes

Notes

Notes

www.ingramcontent.com/pod-product-compliance
Lightning Source LLC
LaVergne TN
LVHW020647100826
845148LV00012B/2356

9781680318333